IDIOCRACY

T0285918

# ZORAN TERZIĆ

# IDIOCRACY
## THE CULTURE OF THE NEW IDIOT

### TRANSLATED FROM THE GERMAN BY
### MICHAEL TURNBULL

DIAPHANES

# TABLE OF CONTENTS

● ○

"There are too many idiots in this world," Frantz Fanon once wrote, acknowledging that his claim required some explanation. For the criteria for declaring someone to be an idiot vary considerably. All idiots look the same from a distance, but from up close you discover something surprising: yourself. Whether "brainless" simpleton or anti-hero ("tall blond man with one black shoe"), whether online troll or drunken tourist, whether fringe political agitator or cultic underminder of everyday consumerism, the idiot doesn't interpret the world before changing it. He is an insensible bearer of meaning, and therefore also a sign of his times. The German playwright Botho Strauß sees him flashing up as the "epitome" of our century. The idiot is the fictitious manifestation of reality, and he is the real manifestation of an economy based on fiction—both as symptom of the mass blindness to power relations and as their saboteur. What does his presence tell us about our present?

"Idiot" was a political term in antiquity, and only began to refer to mental deficiency over time. This book returns to the political origins of idiocy and traces an arc to present-day political sensitivities. It examines the ideological network of individual, conformity, and dissent through the cultural figuration of the idiot: in the first part of the book as *the one* idiot, in the second part as *the many* idiots.

The first part deals with the literary, artistic, ontological roles of the idiot figure. Existential isolation; the mute question of meaning, of world, of all others; numbness, autonomy; lack of restraint and stoic defiance—these are the elements that define the idiot's cultural history.

● ○

Questionable messianic figures abound: geniuses, maniacs, potentates, untouchables … What do these figurations of the idiot reveal to us about the constitution of our self?

In the second part I discuss the idiotization mechanisms of today. I examine the rise of the "new idiot" (Deleuze & Guattari), the exemplifier of a state of mind now being discussed in terms of the singularization, narcissism, and infantilization of a media-savvy society driven by a post-Fordist mode of production. The suggestion here is that there is a new quality of idiocy linked to the politically absurd. The political goons that we have become used to by now aren't the cause but merely the symptom of a deeply rooted self-sabotage—we may find our leaders repugnant, but that's how we want them, because everything is repugnant. In the 1980s the French psychiatrist and philosopher Félix Guattari was writing about a "new ethical-aesthetic paradigm," thus describing the schizophrenic ramification of the law of value through postindustrialized societies, whose subjects see themselves torn between information, surveillance, and cultural capitalism. This points to a late-modern condition I summarize in the term *idiocracy*. I don't refer here to the well known filmic dystopia or to a general mental decline. We aren't getting dumber, rather the opposite: we're getting more creative, more idiosyncratic certainly, but also more confused, when a problem concerns us all at once—be it the climate, a pandemic, a war. Idiocracy can be seen as a futuristic fable about *the rule of the self*. In this fable each of us is a hero or heroine equipped with a task but lacking a goal. We end up running around like idiots, narrow-minded, self-centered, but also chronically self-fulfilled and frenetically "happy." How to analyze today what's so deeply embedded in our global way of life? How to radicalize the perspective that has been laid out, for example, by Christopher Lasch in *The Culture of Narcissism* (1979)? All social criticism will be confronted by a dilemma that Herbert Marcuse pondered in the 1960s: "One-Dimensional Man will vacillate throughout between two contradictory hypotheses: (1) that advanced industrial society is capable of containing qualitative change for the foreseeable future; (2) that forces and tendencies exist which may break this containment and explode the society. I do not think that a clear answer can be given." The more evidence of a condition you collect, the more insurmountable it appears (the problem of structural observation). And the more "flexible" this diagnosis of an era is, the more unserviceable it becomes (the problem of every post-structural observation). There is a "dynamic intractability" in seeing the dilemma itself as part of the diagnosis. Idiocracy reproduces clarity as unclarity, and it creates confusion through a glut of solutions. "Reflexive modernization," as the German sociologist Ulrich Beck once put it, produces crises en masse until we're lost in the hall of mirrors of late modernity and no longer reflect on anything. The greater the production of distraction and blindness, the more improbable the activation of the "post-Fordist multitude" (Paolo Virno), and the more paradoxical the political panorama, with new alliances between the far right and identitarian left, between democrats and autocrats, or between secular liberals and religious fundamentalists. The indissoluble simultaneity of singularity and conformity, risk and safety, clarity and unclarity, ideology and utopia, stagnation and acceleration directs all the energies of the attention economy to the singular person. Individuals appear to be more seducible today than in the 1930s, to judge solely by the follower dynamics on the Internet, but they are seduced in all directions, so there is no apparent susceptibility to old-school totalitarianism. Since individuals are unpredictable, uncontrollable, and to a certain extent "impossible" in their uniqueness, the resulting sociodynamics are both regressive and creative. Something is always being started and destroyed: *start-up, pop-up, blow-up*. The right-wing denialist fights the green economy while profiting from it. The wheelerdealer strives to eliminate his rivals, but counts on them to avert the coming crisis. Competition is brutal, it is said, but deep inside it's paradoxical, and is carried on ontologically, as the apocalyptic preemption of the "only one and its own" (Max Stirner). Even though there's much talk today about global awareness and sustainability, the commons and commonality, in the idiotic whole the solipsism of the isolated subject plays an increasingly important role and is always an aspect in the formation of the "challenged community" (Jean-Luc Nancy), which continues to function even when overchallenged. The isolated self of the many is the new center of the world—an impossible world to which we will nevertheless have to adapt as best we can.

Because any fool can spot another one anywhere today, it's difficult to analyze what makes fools fools, as it impacts the analysis itself. Proclaiming the global reach of the idiot implies that one is above it. Or as Jürgen Habermas puts it: "If there is no such thing as a form of reason that can transcend its own context, then the philosopher who proposes this same picture may not lay claim to a perspective that allows him this overview." We can only face this dilemma with perspectivist reasoning and repeated attempts on the phenomenon, comparable to a sculptor working on a raw piece of wood until something recognizable emerges from it. Yet analysts, like artists, are not unmoved movers. If Saint-Just once said that nobody can rule guiltlessly, this also means that no one with any degree of understanding about what's happening today can distance themselves from it. We're basically all the stooges of an abstract, political-economic giver of meaning—the Holy Spirit of capital—whose global presence is both obvious and inconspicuous as it pervades all areas of society, mutating in time and space. In as much as we are aware of its portents, we are simultaneously aspects of its spectrum of action, and in as much as we are unaware of them, we are under its spell. This essay on the idiot is therefore also an essay on the preconditions for placing oneself outside this spectrum without reproducing the usual gestures of criticism or resistance that are commodified as soon as made. The idiotic is ultimately what can *only* be commodified, or what categorically evades any commodification.

# 1

# THE ONE IDIOT

# ZERO EXPRESSION

*Being an idiot is no box of chocolates.*
Forrest Gump

*If you don't think, you're not stupid*—The idiot's timeless contours aren't only discerned in older literature, whose heroes tilt at windmills. Later writing also draws on simple-mindedness. Imagine an amalgam of William Faulkner's Benjy and Theodore Sturgeon's Lone, add in Dostoyevsky's Myshkin and Flannery O'Connor's Enoch Emery, and complete the mix with Gerhart Hauptman's Emmanuel Quint and Winston Groom's Forrest Gump. A figure emerges of someone rough, backward, and naive, but also oddly self-determined: "Emmanuel stood there, his arms hanging at his sides, an immobile expression on his colorless face, which was neither challenging nor intimidated" (Hauptmann). This expression becomes the object of intellectual interest. Flaubert writes in passing that the face of an imbecile stimulates thoughtfulness. The idiot is a zero, but not a passive one. Botho Strauß sees in him "the fragment of a deep, powerful typology." So there's something there. The idiot is animated by a task whose objectives are clear to him alone. Like Sturgeon's Lone he never asks why anything happens, and like Faulkner's Benjy he is indiscriminately aware of past and present. Sometimes giving the impression of "brainlessness," the idiot grows new mental organs that push to the surface. Enoch Emery has "wise blood." He needs no emotional guidance or intellectual deduction, as he has an inborn knowledge of how to lead his life. He doesn't have to draw conclusions, for all conclusions have already been drawn. True is what's there. What isn't there isn't true. The simpleton lives in the plainest of all worlds. Unlike Voltaire's Candide, who ultimately cultivates his garden, Emery makes off in a stolen gorilla costume. If you have a clear conscience, doubt is replaced by any action: *dubito ergo dubito, cogito ergo cogito*. I doubt, therefore I doubt; I think, therefore I think. *Ergo sum* isn't the utmost sentiment here. And the state of affairs, and with it any other state of affairs, is as clear as clarity itself. —And so here ends my book.

*Numb gaze*—The idiot's motivation, however, remains a mystery: is he urged to action by mental deficiency, or is he made by blind will? What comprises his pathological core? In literature the debility of the idiot is a vehicle for anchoring him in the world as a transcendental observer. As a *prima persona* he looks at his surroundings with fresh eyes and exposes the common idiocy of ordinary people. The dementia ascribed to him spares us the explanation of what the idiot really is and how his thinking comes about as thinking, or of the insight conveyed by thinking that isn't thinking. Faulkner therefore puts Benjy as a mentally retarded narrator at the start of his novel, which anticipates the fractures of a family drama in his faltering account. Benjy's savant ability to smell far-reaching events from a distance allows his organ of thought to entangle with the Southern magic. What remains at the end of the story is the numb gaze of the idiot settling over the landscape. As Woyzeck's Doctor diagnoses: "Facial muscles rigid, taut, occasional twitches. Condition strained, excitable."

Johann Caspar Lavater, *Portrait of an "Idiot"* (detail), 1792.

*Internal life*—The zero expression of the idiot is related to staring at the screen. The idiot "gawks." In Georg Büchner we read of "Viehsionomik," a pun on livestock (*Vieh*) and physiognomy, and in the meme universe the idiot has a "derp face," the mockery of a face. The idiot's zero expression isn't blank but vague. It can similarly be seen in moments of nervous stress or drunkenness. The American neuroendocrinologist Robert Sapolsky has compared the various expressive qualities of physical states to a strongly beating heart: physiologically it isn't possible to make out whether someone is having an orgasm or about to commit a murder. It's the same with the figurations of idiotic expression: it can't always be established whether a pathology is manifested or a radical trait or both at the same time. Such ambiguity is seen in savants, whose descriptive condition has historically fluctuated between "idiot savant" (John Langdon Down) and "islands of genius" (Darold A. Treffert). The works of artistically gifted savants circulate between galleries and medical journals because no one understands the basis of autistic expression. The originator of the term autism, the Swiss psychiatrist Eugen Bleuler, spoke of "internal life." Since then the psychopathological debate has apparently been about states of consciousness and how they are linked to the social exterior. But "linked" is an unreliable expression here, for there is no one connecting or conveying anything here. The literary or artistic fascination with the figure of the idiot derives from the liminal experience that manifests in these states. "What if it is the illness then?" asks Myshkin, "if the end-result, the instant of apprehension, [...] turns out to be the highest pitch of harmony and beauty, conferring a sense of some hitherto unknown and unguessed completeness, proportion, reconciliation, an ecstatic, prayerful fusion with the supreme synthesis of life?" The zero expression has nothing to do with unconsciousness, but rather—as with pilot training—with the threshold between unconsciousness and consciousness, with undertaking permanent attempts to be "there." We can imagine the idiot at this brink: mindlessness as a form of consciousness; unconsciousness as a way of being. And that's what art wants too. But so does the economy. It's what everyone wants. Everyone wants to be an idiot, the *homo ex animo* as the truth of *homo oeconomicus*.

*Human-like*—The zero expression is synchronized with its physical impulses. Idiots are driven by an outside force which paradoxically originates within them. This is why in literature the idiot is a Janus-faced figure. He is either a passive piece of nature—"animals in human form," as the eighteenth-century French physician and philosopher Julien de La Mettrie called idiots—or a willful and reasonable human being who stands further out from this nature than others. Both forms imply isolated minds. Writers with a sense of the idiotic use psychopathology both clinically and metaphorically, so as to play off the idiot's will against his passivity. The Austrian avant-garde poet Konrad Bayer describes the figures in his play *idiot* (1960) as "human-like beings." They make short work of everything that stands in their way: the protagonist, called *idiot a*, kills other beings, drives a lawnmower over their corpses, collects the remnants in a bag, which he takes away and then drops. Then: "suddenly a human-like being appears on the periphery | although *a* doesn't seem to notice, he jumps up and kicks the guy from the stage with astonishing agility and utter expressionlessness" (Bayer). At one point a human being encounters *idiot a*: "brother!" says the human being expectantly, but *a* knocks him down straight away and tears out his arms. It turns out that the human being, with his "load of crap" (culture, art, feelings, history, idealism, reason, state, etc.) is a part of *a*. The idiot has no use for real humans, because they are an exterior part of his being, and his interior being is pure action. There is no reason for anything. Reason is felled as soon as it arises.

*Unrivaled*—Not all idiots who perfect their zero expression into a zero action are as violent as Bayer's *idiot a*. Dostoyevsky's Myshkin is a good person through and through, and this he is only able to be because he is ill, because he doesn't have everyone else's standard health. If you are unrivaled, you sense the spectacle of the *conditio humana* from up close, and not like everyone else from a distance. Hence "the study of idiocy is the study of a particular form of exile" (Patrick McDonagh). This configuration is found throughout cultural history. The blockbuster GUARDIANS OF THE GALAXY (2014) features the humanoid tree being Groot, who is similar to the tree being in Andrea Mantegna's *Triumph of the Virtues* (1502). In the Marvel universe Groot is an outcast from his world because of his good nature. Mantegna's tree being protects the Temple of Virtue. In order to save the universe, Groot joins forces with other freaks who also have special talents. Like Sturgeon's idiots and Mantegna's, they become the guardians of humankind. In the manner of Mantegna's panel painting, the Hollywood universe invokes a moral code that becomes a matrix of the Christian crusade of good against evil. Groot is now the good guy among good guys. He possesses unique powers that assign him the role of heroic simpleton. Mantegna's tree being is enveloped by a scroll bearing a pseudo-script repeating the same sentence in different languages. And Groot's communication consists only of the sentence "I am Groot." In the end this one-phrase wonder becomes the savior of the universe.

*First and last reasons*—The idiot emphasizes a certain ontological equanimity in his or her actions that differs from what Martin Heidegger called the "free air of the high heavens." The idiot's expression arises in the shallow acceptance of negativity. It doesn't shun nothingness or less than nothingness; it goes for more stagnation when things are already stagnant. "No desire. No certainty. More of a floral existence: simple opening to the light. Without expecting the end. Warmed by the unforeseeable," as Botho Strauß observes. Hölderlin gets to the heart of it in the nocturne "Timidity": "Go then, my soul, into life | Naked, without anxiety." Myshkin experiences something similar before his epileptic fit: "His mind and heart were bathed in an extraordinary illumination. All his agitation, all his doubts and anxieties, seemed to be instantly reconciled and resolved into a lofty serenity, filled with pure, harmonious gladness and hope, filled too with the consciousness of the ultimate cause of all things." The zero expression contains a spectrum of emphases; it reflects the light of the ordinary as if through a prism.

*Pre-face*—An equivalent to this expression can be found in Pascal Claude's 1954 preface to the catalogue of a series of paintings by Yves Klein. It shows blank lines:

———————————————————————————————

———————————————————————————————

———————————————————————————————

———————————————————————————————

But they aren't really blank; they are "fully" there as a poetic zero statement. They form a kind of communicative antecedent; no interface, they are a *pre-face* to the declaration. "The poetic language the idiot has in mind [...] knows that the prelingual is also generated by language," writes the German poet Monika Rinck in her book *Risk and Idiocy* (2019). What for the poet is transcendental textual similarity is for the idiot transcendental humanoid similarity. The pre-face that stares out of language is only expressionless in the sense that no expression can do justice to the solemnity of real experience—in this case of art. From this perspective the zero expression is a prefiguration, a face before itself. Tracing the many faces of the world back to a single face: *that* brings about the stirrings of the idiot.

*Enigma*—Humanoid beings know without *sensing* their knowledge, and they sense it without knowing it. Idiots, in their rawness, attain a sublimity that can never be reached by the intellect, which must bow, as for example in John Cleland's *Fanny Hill* (1748), to the laconic "rhetoric of the penis" (Mark Blackwell). In this erotic novel the imbecile Dick has such an aroused member as to discompose the prostitute Louise enough to abandon her profession. And Charles Bukowski's Henry from *The Last Night of the Earth* (1992), who decides to become an idiot at the age of eleven, believes himself in possession of the finest erection in Los Angeles. The fact that male fantasies are closely tied to idiocy can hardly be denied here, but how are we to grasp all the other centrifugal forces of the idiot? Botho Strauß writes: "The idiot presents an enigma. That is, he retains his share of the mysterious, which the rest of the world, having long enjoyed a wealth of it, lost to the fervor of riddle-solvers. But he can be seen as an emblem of that principally inadequate understanding of the world to which the human species is condemned."

# TOUR D'IDIOT—
# A HISTORY OF THE PECULIAR PERSON

*Such items are called individuals because each of them is consti-*
*tuted of proper features [idiotes] the assemblage [athroisma] of*
*which will never be the same in anything else.*

Porphyry

*Idion*—Idiocy once referred to the uniqueness of things. *Idion* is what is particular, what is its own by its own measure. An idiot is someone with qualities distinct from the usual. The protagonists of Lars von Trier's film THE IDIOTS (1998) refer to this when they talk of "bringing out your inner idiot." You should be your own idiot, not the idiot of others, a useless idiot, not a useful one. The uniqueness shouldn't be forced, but should come from within, sometimes appearing as the "inner swine." Where and what is this within? Which animal species occupies its symptomatic space? An interior cultural history emerges parallel to the exterior, just as human history can also be parsed as a metazoological narrative, from Jean Renoir's "human beast" to Nietzsche's "otherwise animal," that is, the other, inner, unfathomable, humanoid of the human being that remains enigmatic even after it has been scientifically understood. The unexplained shooting spree always follows the one that has been explained. There's just enough obscuration in every explanation for the enigma to remain. Genetics or brain research are raising new questions about free will that are leading to old-new assertions that are raising new-old questions in turn. Asserters can do nothing other than continually produce conceptual explosives they can't defuse. It goes on and on, with no end to the riddle. The explained human would no longer be human but a *homo stans*, indistinguishable from a thing. This is why von Trier takes a profane approach: he doesn't assert and doesn't explain; he portrays a group of dropouts who live in a communal house and act being mentally retarded in public. Neighbors and passers-by are coaxed into the role of assistants or doctors, and participate in redefining the world. The commune shows that it's no longer the idealist or the revolutionary but apparently only the idiot who is able to throw off conventions—or as Möbius puts it in Friedrich Dürrenmatt's *The Physicists* (1961): "Only in the madhouse can we still be free. Only in the madhouse can we still afford to think." Whether you're really an idiot or just acting is irrelevant, as *it's nevertheless idiotic to be it*. We act ourselves into mindlessness; we rationalize ourselves into a rage. The call to "bring out your inner idiot" is a call not to stupidity but to freedom, that is, to strive for a unique life that makes sense beyond liberal hedonism or bourgeois identity. Free animal, unfree beast. The theme of the idiot speaks to the history of both mental outsiderness and the artist collective. In this respect von Trier's communards are the descendants of Myshkin. But along with the segregation of the idiot, the game of freedom, in which "reason automatically threatens to plunge into madness" (Michel Foucault), also brings to light the idiotisms of society, whose shallow reflection it is. For idiots are "brought out" everywhere, it's just that the consequences aren't always liberating. On the contrary, modern technocracy continually reproduces the idiocy and "infinite stupidity of the masses" (Gustave Flaubert), which has merged into the speculative nature of the modern economy. This is why the communards seek the idiotic confrontation, similarly to the Dadaist, "who as a madman toys with the madness of society," as the German anthropologist Constantin von Barloewen comments. And after a Venetian carnival procession passed his window, Goethe concluded that "freedom and equality can only be enjoyed in the frenzy of madness." Today it seems as if this sound has taken on a life of its own to become the cosmic background noise of our current societies.

*Fools*—Historically, the idiot can often be seen in the role of a figure strutting on the periphery of the center of power, a role inhabited by tricksters, jesters, pranksters, ingénues, or fools in a situation where their distinct qualities can take effect. Many of these figures are united in being able to behave in ways that would be proscribed elsewhere, meaning a sphere as yet undefined by them. This subversive leeway can most clearly be seen in the relationship to monarchic power. Court jesters aren't literally "idiots," nevertheless their oddity protects them from becoming a serious threat to the court. These subjects—from the physically disabled freak to the astute philosopher—are witty bodies whose deployment confirms the irony of power as power. All very contemporary: political trolls, scandal celebs, comedians, public intellectuals, or It girls now occupy these archaic positions, which always reflect, embrace, or pass on something of power. The "inner idiot" of universal foolery is acted out through all available means and needs no mandate, even when the slapstick is decreed. But what is done is just done, without being subject to the libidinous, epistemological, or economic order, as von Barloewen observes: "When the court jester Morot was walking next to the king under the royal canopy as the rain poured down, and his majesty haughtily gave him to understand that he could not suffer a fool at his side, Morot swiftly replied, 'But I can!'"

*Lucky thought*—Coquetry with a deficit that is turned into an asset has its own history. In his late dialogues, Nicholas of Cusa imagines himself as a philosophical amateur, whom he calls Idiota, in order to rail against the theological mainstream in a modern reformulation, as *docta ignorantia,* of the Socratic method of heavily ironic not-knowing. Knowledge is power, ignorance an art: the unread simpleton is wiser than the distinguished philosopher because he is free from the usual formulae of thought. "I do know that no one's authority guides me, even if it attempts to influence me," declares Idiota. And so this gay scientist thinks what he thinks, and can easily take on the roundabout teachings of the scholastics. "The mind, in looking unto its own simplicity, beholds all things in simplicity and apart from compositeness," announces Idiota, in a challenge to the universal "stupidity of cleverness" (Theodor W. Adorno). Nicholas sees through the performance of knowledge as power in his populist thinker. Idiota earns his living by carving wooden spoons, and derives all his insights from this craft. He is the mathematical opposite of the polymath, and yet the listening philosopher expresses his admiration for the fact that Idiota reproduces knowledge from the schools of Aristotle and Plato. Indeed, philosophers had always wanted to philosophize like Idiota. Didn't his carving of spoons have something of the razor-sharp reasoning visible in the sculpture of thought? A thought, as much as it deserves the name, was something well formed. Nicholas contrasts what was called *prudentia* in ancient Rome with *scientia*: wisdom against knowledge, synthesis against circumstance, the occurrence of knowledge against the knowledge of occurrence. His Idiota begins *beneath stupidity*. He has something that the trickster and divine envoy Hermes was supposed to have had before him: the "inner knowledge of all things" (Lewis Hyde). The intellect, for Idiota, is not something that unfolds; on the contrary, it is the figuratively and conceptually elusive "image of the Eternal Enfolding," as Nicholas of Cusa puts it. The language of the amateur has no claims to transcendence and is unbeholden to any milieu. Nicholas introduces the biblical image of "wisdom in the streets" and has his men of learning marvel at a passing group of pilgrims, who confidently reach their destination without common accord. Idiota is an individual, a one-off, on whom the light has fallen. Descartes will later talk of "natural light" and give Idiota's role to Eudoxos. Deleuze and Guattari also refer to this figure in their definition of the idiot as a "notional person," a fictive person in whom the real thoughts of the philosophers live. Here they reactivate the ancient concept in late-modern thought: "The idiot," they write, "is the private thinker, in contrast to the public teacher (the schoolman) [...] a very strange type of persona who wants to think, and who thinks for himself, by the 'natural light.'" Light and lamp, enlightenment, illumination, luminosity. These are the metaphors for an insight that springs from the most primitive source of energy—a "bioenergy" of sorts. Simple recognition straight from the earth, no need for power stations and disposal sites, the way Angelus Silesius's rose blooms "without why." Self-sufficient, effortlessly, demanding nothing beyond one's due, expecting and requiring nothing, like Sturgeon's idiot Lone, not even the transvaluation of values— zero measure, zero ethics. With Angelus Silesius this is a divine state that does without ontological difference. Without worry, without fear, without joy, without calm, without boredom, without tension, without emptiness, without grief, and—going further than Socrates—without "reason." Idiota is not privileged, but he has the ability to explain the world without intellectual contortions or specialist jargon—*idiota doctus*, learned fool, Accatone. But how is this at all possible? Doesn't his knowledge arise from mere whim, and is he not right by mere coincidence? This assumption may make sense later, but not now. Idiotic serendipity reflects the everyday experience of evidence: insight shouldn't be something imposed by the thinker, but rather something that arises of its own accord—both by chance and necessarily. Nicholas's experts are bewildered by the way in which an arbitrary person is effortlessly able to outsmart them, but they are even more astounded to recognize themselves the lumpenproletariat of reason.

*Dysfunction*—Contrarian without a thought, troublemaker without a mission. The road of the wise amateur Idiota to the present-day insult "Idiot!" is a winding one. It begins where the *idion* has a social effect, where it becomes the symptom of failure. In ancient Athens *idiotes* was referred to a "private person," someone who only took care of his personal affairs and was therefore unsuited to the business of state. In antiquity the term was often used functionally, for example as the political opposite of *strategos*, as a term for the prosaist rather than the poet, to denote the amateur, or to identify bureaucratic matters (private and public sacrificial rites were charged at different rates, for example). Politically, *idiotes* meant a dysfunction. In the *Laws* Plato writes that "public good binds together states, but private only distracts them." A society of private persons is impossible because there can be no arbitration of all individual interests and the political logos can't encompass the rationality of all its actors. Put differently: you can't please everyone if everyone is already right in his own way—in ancient eyes the utopian fulfilment of this aim would be a society in the singular, an *idiocracy*. Christian philosophy of the state later introduced the governmental technique of "pastoral power" (Foucault) as the arbitrator between the individual demanding his right and the right of the many: the shepherd takes care of the herd as a whole and of the welfare of the individual sheep. If necessary the individual is sacrificed to ensure the welfare of all, but all the others may also be sacrificed to ensure the welfare of the individual: "*Omnes et singulatim*. The paradox of the shepherd" (Foucault). This technique of subjectivation has become secularized in modernity, leading to our late-capitalist condition in which the interests of the state and individual maintain a complex interrelationship. The question of how and when the "era of governmentality" (Foucault) leads to the *era of the idiot* is underpinned by an era-encompassing tension between the individual and state, idiocy and policy.

*Self-sabotage*—In 2005, a decade before Donald J. Trump aimed for office, the American educationalist Walter C. Parker warned against the far-reaching consequences of idiotization, which he sees emerging in the ubiquitous hype of the private. The private isn't the same as the individual; people call their property private even when everyone owns the same cellphones or wears the same caps. According to Parker, the inflation of the private necessarily leads to a general disorientation, a problem that can be traced back to antiquity. Plato called it ideopragy (*idiopragia*), meaning action following a self-calibrated compass taking place on a rudderless ship that is about to crash onto the rocks. What in today's entrepreneur-driven societies with its space billionaires and superhero cultural icons appears as a virtue is in the ancient frame of reference something that must be overcome, as "human nature will be always drawing him into avarice and selfishness, [...] and so working darkness in his soul will at last fill with evils both him and the whole city" (Plato). Avarice is idiotic when it turns into its opposite and makes paupers of the greedy. The entrepreneur driven by the prospect of his own advantage advances his own loss. There is Marxian dialectic in the Platonic here: the author of *Capital* (1867) would write of the "idiotism of the bourgeois world" predicated on a matrix of downfall. The modern interpretation of ideopragy is a judicial formula, however, describing an equitable division of labor in the formation of the state based on the specific abilities of each individual. Marx's free future society is inspired by this: "From each according to his abilities, to each according to his needs." The idiotism to which Marx refers is the fact that the abilities and needs of the bourgeoisie express an alienated desire that ultimately turns against the self-actualization of each individual—something that incidentally can also be said for the later reinterpretation of the above slogan as the socialist performance principle, namely "to each according to his work."

*Isolated*—The insights of Marx and Plato have lost none of their relevance, for neither are today's societies idiot-proof. In certain US states citizens officially declared idiots are not entitled to vote. The idiots in question aren't the lobbyists of powerful corporations who have asserted their "special interests" but persons with extremely low IQs. This link between idiocy and "dysrationalia" (Keith Stanovitch) was established by nineteenth-century psychiatry. In 1801 Philippe Pinel published the first standard work to systemize mental illnesses, the *Traité médico-philosophique sur l'aliénation mentale*. This tract distinguished between five groups: melancholics, monomaniacs, maniacs, dotards, and idiots. Pinel's decisive contribution was the formulation of a distinct psychopathology for each illness, that is, the different maladies weren't manifestations of one and the same madness, but had to be treated in different departments. The concept of idiotism referred to the consequences of physiological abnormalities (such as "small-headedness," or microcephaly), but was also understood in a more abstract sense that went beyond the horizon of ordinary illness. One of the studies subsequent to Pinel, on *Insanity in Relation to Medicine and State Pharmacology* (1863) by Jean-Étienne-Dominique Esquirol, asserts that "idiocy is not an illness but a state in which the intellectual capacities never existed or were unable to develop." The distinction between "illness" and "state" is important in order to emphasize the singularity of the idiot. "The word *idios, privatus, solitarius* expresses the state of a person who, robbed of reason, stands alone, as it were, sequestered from the rest of nature" (Esquirol). But this nature of the idiot is normatively undermined from the start, and also implies "culture." Esquirol describes the case of a patient suffering from idiocy, whom he recommended to "get on a horse" for relaxation. He later found out that the patient had taken this recommendation literally and had sat on a horse for hours without moving from the spot. The literal implementation fell short of the therapy but fulfilled the purpose, for it was apparently relaxing for the patient to sit on a horse without riding off. But all the neurologist can see in this intellectual spontaneity is the symptom of an isolated mind. Michel Foucault compiled such cases in order to illustrate the discrepancy between medical analysis and the experience of imprisonment. In this context he wrote that "madness, at bottom, was only possible in so far as it had that latitude around it, the leeway that allowed the subject to speak the language of his own madness, and constitute himself as mad." This is the "culture" of the idiot. Authority sets up common-sense variables for behavior. The patient doesn't recognize or understand these variables and takes the words literally. Like an idiot, for sure, but not the doctor's idiot—like his *own* idiot. It is *his* act that nobody has predicted. And the doctor is as untreatable as his patient, not because he's sick, but in the same way that a God may be almighty but unable to believe in God, that is, he blinds himself to a categorical possibility. The idiotism of the doctor is never an issue, because all the patient's acts are pathologically defined from the start, and I don't deny that there are good reasons for this. I only emphasize, in reference to Clément Rosset, that idiotism *continues to exist* above or beneath illness as a *metaphysical, performative* or *phantasmal fact.* My analysis appeals to this variety. So for the above example it would be possible to say that both entities participate in the same *idiot type,* but playing different roles in the confrontation. The doctor utilizes a language game; the patient draws his attention to it. And this in turn describes a model for philosophical work on the concept of the idiot.

*Nexus*—Until the fourteenth century the term "idiot" still carried the meaning of "private individual." Despite the depoliticization of the concept in the following centuries, certain characteristics still remain: the isolation and singularity of the mind, the self-foundation. One interpretation for this continuity is that in the course of the eighteenth-century enlightenment movement the *idiotes*, in the form of the self-founded individual, became the heart of the modern social contract, while other aspects of the term became useful in clinical diagnostics. For even an individual based on natural law is separate from the rest of nature. Rousseau therefore called infants perfect idiots. In this sense the individual is only a person when he is also an idiot, as Adorno puts it, "sealed and split off from society." In the modern period an increasing atomization of the social order, with its "microphysics of power" (Foucault), brings about the idiot as an irreducible entity of politics. So while John Locke gives the idiot the role of a non-person who renders the social contract inoperative and must therefore be excluded from the social group (and whose property and body may be confiscated by the kingdom, and so forth), another aspect of the idiot, identified by Rousseau, is the very precondition for the social contract, in that morals and politics rest on the foundations of a natural subject understood as existing for itself; in that the *idiotes*, seen in ancient Greece as the opposite of political reason, becomes the basis of the social order. In other words, the mental illness of the idiot is constituted similarly to the political health of the *citoyen*. Both draw on the same idea. The attraction of the term "idiot" is that it speaks to all these different spheres, for the underground nexus of private and moronic has apparently disappeared from political discourse and the (a)political idiot been replaced by other terms—otherwise *only* idiots could vote and *only* idiots could be voted for, the "populist" way. Nevertheless the relationship remains: people who refer only to themselves have their own viewpoint, but they underestimate the inherent facts of the task in hand, and at the same time overestimate their own expertise; they become learned idiots. Ultimately the idiot—whether clueless or learned, with a high or low IQ—will fail. Today's high-tech entrepreneurs or financial jugglers may look "individual" or "enlightened" from outside, but in regard to their social surplus value they're as much on the rampage as the monomaniac in the nineteenth-century madhouse. The walls of the locked institution have simply been put up around the planet.

*Hatchers*—What does it mean, in reference to Plato and Marx, to politicize the concept of the idiot once again and to redetermine its planetary reach? What Deleuze & Guattari write about the history of philosophy also applies to the history of the idiot, which is "completely without interest if it does not undertake to awaken a dormant concept and to play it again on a new stage, even if this comes at the price of turning it against itself." Awakening the concept means embracing it from all sides, using it as a tool to discuss a contemporary social paradox, namely the fact that increasing isolation and increasing herd behavior are one and the same thing, as social media illustrate every day. Usual dichotomies such as private/public, I/world, self/other, individual/mass, individual/dividual, and so on must be re-defined in "idiological" terms, that is, from the point of view of the idiot as a transcendental figure. "The idiots sit on the century to hatch it— they start all over a few centuries later," wrote the Dadaist poet Tristan Tzara. Has the time come round again?

*Egonomics*—Contemporary social analysis focuses not so much on the idiotism in politics as on egoism, profit-making from other people's misery. But where self-interest is reversed it gives rise to an idiot driven by "disinterested liking," to put it in Kantian terms. The typical egoist wants the best for himself at all times, and unlike the idiot he never acts alone. In *The Poverty of Philosophy* (1847) Marx writes: "Every egoism operates in society and by the fact of society. Hence it presupposes society, that is to say, common aims, common needs, common means of production, etc., etc." The careerist moves with his opportunities, the idiot against them. "When an 'idiot,' a selfless person, falls into the world of egoists, it can only end badly," concludes a recent review of a stage version of Dostoyevsky's novel. Egoists ensure their backs are covered, but idiots jump out of the plane without a golden parachute. They simply like jumping. The visual language of Martin Scorsese's THE WOLF OF WALL STREET (2013) comes to mind here, with its concentrically intertwining investments and injections, securities and prostitutes. The monetary economist Willem Buiter coined the term "cognitive regulatory capture" for "the process through which those in charge of the relevant state entity internalise and adopt, as if by osmosis, the objectives, interests, fears, hopes and perception of reality of the vested sectional interest they are meant to regulate." In Adam McKay's film THE BIG SHORT (2015) this cognitive state failure is reflected in the figure of a financial-regulation official amusing herself in a Las Vegas pool with a broker from Goldman Sachs. The libido accomplishes its own family constellation—the marriage of the regulator and the regulated. McKay was also wise enough to portray the essence of the financial crisis in a Idiota-like freak at its epicenter: Dr. Michael Berry, the cranky one-eyed financial wizard, is the first to sense the coming collapse because his idiot-instinct is synchronized with the general economic drift. Idiota has his wooden spoon, Berry his heavy-metal drum sticks. Berry's unmusical colleagues are unable to perceive the economic reality of the looming real-estate crisis, and they revile him as an amateur because he sees the subprime market stirring while everyone else is wallowing in the mud of economic equilibrium. This is the idiot factor, the level that starts below stupidity—the ego that gives birth to its own id: opaque instincts interwoven with interests for which the phrase "greed for profit" is inadequate. Greed is a symptom of the egoist, who follows clearly defined goals. The idiot acts more subliminally and contradictorily. He spins out the everyday until it has universal meaning and the logical structure of instinct is equivalent to speculation—capital-driven "animals in human form." In a political or economic crisis the totality of this level of meaning becomes clear, and an alternative order and social perspective emerges: when today's financial experts praise labor-market flexibilization with reference to animal instincts, they forget that these very instincts demand the total collapse. Welcome to the cognitive capture of the real.

## THE TWO REALMS OF THE IDIOT

*Isolation & crowds*—In the character of the lofty sage or unwitting hero, the idiot is a refined, zeroed figure. In the character of the lout, the dolt, the drunken tourist, the babbling conspiracy theorist, the idiot is primarily body, and in Jean-Luc Nancy's sense speaks the language of the body. The ontological difference hasn't yet filtered through to the idiot. He is "a torn-off rose in the determined gush of people" (Botho Strauß), but he also corresponds to the sea of flowers mass-produced under glass; he is a residuum of mass idiotization. For Gilles Deleuze the idiot stands for the virtue of speechlessness, the inaptitude of a statement. Yes, but the idiot also never stops talking, confiding, thinking it necessary to comment on everything online. For Byung-Chul Han the idiot is "unallied, un-networked, and uninformed. The idiot inhabits the immemorial outside, which escapes communication and networking altogether." Yes, but the idiot is also *exclusively* networked, and merges into the social medium as a "power user." For Avital Ronell idiots "appear to be organized by pre-ethical impulses that prompt unreflected acts of compassion." Yes, but idiots are also those social-justice warriors or bourgeoise activists exclusively driven by ethical impulses who stumble into a world beyond good and evil. When "joy knows no bounds," it can be as idiotic as boundless seriousness. So our *tour d'idiot* traverses two realms:

(1) That of the instinctual private thinker, of the airy nature-boy, the reluctant troublemaker, the simple sage, the subversive Idiota, the inspired amateurs and dazed outsider nerds, who unconsciously upend the knowledge of their time. I call all these *idiot types of the first order* or, more broadly, I place them in the *first realm of the idiot*;

(2) That of the overenthusiastic lout, dull ignoramus, ruthless profiteer, self-assertive fanatic or self-sabotaging freak, who pulls the world down into the abyss after him. The cursed idiot of today appears in this realm. I call all these *idiot types of the second order* or, more broadly, I place them in the *second realm of the idiot*.

The division is justified by its precursors. Erasmus speaks of "two sorts of madness," in his *Praise of Folly*, and the literature of fools often throws up bipolar characters: "One court jester lay in front of a golden-framed mirror and closed his eyes so as not to have to see himself sleeping. Another fool raised the leaden anchor of a wooden ship while it was sinking" (von Barloewen). On the one hand only certain types of idiot function like fools; on the other the whole world is foolish, as Bakhtin describes in his study of Rabelais, for example. Regarding the dissolution of reason, Foucault distinguishes between a *cosmic* and a *critical* experience of madness, and here the critical belongs in the first realm of the idiot, as it manifests "a secret life and a source of strength."

*Enigmas*—Idiotypes of the first order are solitaries with special status. You don't encounter them; they are *discovered*. They appear odd to those for whom oddity is a chance quality. What exactly they are, where they come from, where they're going is unclear. In the case of the American Benjaman Kyle, the man with no memory who was found naked in 2004 and whose identity remained mysterious for years, the question of origin was a matter of forensics. But in earlier centuries the question was more fundamental, namely what a human being in an isolated state actually was. In the eighteenth and nineteenth centuries Victor de L'Aveyron and other feral children were examined by scientists interested in a primordial human state discussed by Rousseau and described by Büchner in *Woyzeck* (1836): the human "animal," *l'homme isolé*, a mystery of his time, as Kaspar Hauser's gravestone proclaims, a *homo ferus*, a stranger like Percival living out his days as a "pure soul" far from civilization. The debate around the "born idiot" of Aveyron gave rise to the suspicion that idiocy could have cultural origins. Dostoyevsky took this oscillation between nature and culture as the model for his idiot, whom he lifted from the sanatorium and placed in worldly society as a figure of salvation. His idea, as he wrote in a letter to his niece, was to create a positive amalgam of goodliness and ridiculousness, Christ and Don Quixote in one. In art and literature, over the centuries, this combination of purity and simplemindedness established the *dispositif* of the creative genius. Artists appear all the more relevant in this realm the more isolated, intuitive, and presuppositionless their actions, and ideally, at the beginning of their careers, when they are "discovered" like the feral children of the nineteenth century. Their nakedness is mesmerizing, and it's to everybody's advantage if they don't know what they're doing and how they do it—a theme reverberating in art and literature from the *poète maudit*, the Fauves to the Young British Artists. They are the inspired freaks, sometimes living in squalor on the outskirts, at any rate anti-academic, like Alfred Jarry riding his bicycle through Paris and taking potshots at the smug establishment with his pistol (a gesture that André Breton would later regard as the most basic act of surrealism). Raw, idiotic, for sure, but taking on a sublime form secretly superior to all other states of being. But they don't just include, say, the naive painter, and their aim in general is to return the world to a pristine condition. This tendency is also reflected in the cultural trend of the outsider, as in *art brut*, which encompasses the visionary art of the mad from Adolf Wölfli to Henry Darger, Jim Shaw's collection of thrift-store paintings, or Irwin Chusid's study of outsider music. A parallel strand are the artistic savants, who have formed a category of their own since Gottfried Mind (1768–1814), the "Raphael of cats," and are no longer treated as *idiots savants*, but only located on the pathological spectrum. The range is very wide here, from the primitive art of the sane to the complex art of the mentally ill.

*The naked subject*—This phenomenology of the uncommon may explain the art-world hype of outsiders like Henry Darger, whose fictive world reaches a point beyond art and non-art. On his death Darger left tens of thousands of pages of text and images in his cramped apartment, depicting a fantasy world with child-slave rebellions and epic battles involving young girls with penises. Darger's legacy is preserved in an art museum, not a criminal archive or a mental institution, but isn't there also a forensic interest here in the human enigma, as it cavorts in what Adorno called the "enigma" of art. From painter prince to artist freak, the question of humanity always arises where the art public is confronted with "naked" subjects devoid of middle class frills. From this generalization of the avant-garde on the margins of the psyche and society comes the idea of finally attaining the unpretentious ground of creation: naked and bloody, ordinary and undiscerning, yet accepting the diversity of the world as one. You'll only reveal your deeper understanding if you're discovered. And if you aren't discovered it will remain unspoken, lost in the "sunken place" of reason, as Oliver Sacks describes it in "The Autist Artist" (1985). How much empirical knowledge has been lost by ignoring a minor character?—"Have you found Jesus?" Forrest Gump is asked. "I didn't know I was supposed to be looking for him."

*Dictatorship of the self*—Numinous interest in the loner has persisted into the present, despite postmodern irony, following Ad Reinhardt's dictum, "Art is art-as-art, and everything else is everything else." No outside motivation, still less politics, should be your guide, just art itself, which is everything and nothing. "Everything is nothing," asserts Andy Warhol, provided that "nothing" is art. Pure art is pure idiocy, is the "dictatorship of idiocy," because it gives itself orders so as to be able to fulfil an end in itself. The artist becomes a synthesis of dictator and servant, positivist and nihilist, petit bourgeois and bohemian. So there, before and after art, is the first realm of the idiot. Everything plays out in the idiot, without progressing beyond the artist: "A system with its own set of rules, entitled to everything, legitimized on its own terms," reads a review of Anne Imhof's contribution to the Venice Biennale 2017. And Paul Valéry's "pure poetry" makes no less a claim: "I don't construct a 'System'—My system is me." This self-legitimation, stemming from the time when Giorgio Vasari laid out the biographies of Renaissance painters and thus created the enigma of the artistic subject, extends to the present day. It also applies to the work's inherent logic. Consider Georges Perec's decision to leave out the letter E in one of his novels (a Dadaist idea). There is a hidden connection between the Jacobins turning the calendrical system inside out and the avant-garde doing away with representation.

Bas Jan Ader, *Broken Fall (Organic)*, 1971.

*Spunk*—There are many instances of the self-discovery of the artist as idiot: in KEEP YOUR RIGHT UP (1987) Jean-Luc Godard presents himself as the drummer August immersed in reading Dostoyevsky. In LA RICOTTA (1962) the figure of the director can be read as Pier Paolo Pasolini himself: played by Orson Welles, the cultural hero reads out lines from Pasolini's MAMMA ROMA (1962) and is overwhelmed by his own greatness. In 1988 Julian Schnabel also put down a self-marker by placing a sculpture of signs with the inscription "Idiota" in the courtyard of a deserted castle ruin. The word had been presented on a marble slab by Salvo (Salvatore Mangione) at an exhibition in the 1970s. The dialectic play of inner idiot and shallow amateurism with cultural greatness can also be seen in the work of Roman Signer. Here the aim is to discover active naivety and inquisitive ignorance within oneself—where Socrates once discovered autotelic goodness—not knowing, but endowed with a certain instinct for simple questions. Signer catapults tables and chairs out of "Villa Villekulla" with the aid of explosives. And another cultural heroine, Pippi Longstocking, walks down the street—like Socrates did—asking everyone for a *spunk*. But nobody knows what it is. Neither does Pippi, because she has just invented it ("I make my world how I like it"). It is the luck of airy idiots not to be so overwhelmed by their own knowledge that they can't be surprised by it.

*Gentle idiocy*—Seeing the world through the eyes of the child had a so-cial-revolutionary veneer in the 1960s of the Lindgren screen adapta-tions. The bourgeoisie had no time for Mr. Nilsson, the smart queer monkey who lives on equal footing in Pippi's villa commune. In the modern era this monkey-gaze was recurrently associated with a physi-ological defect: childishness and animality as complimentary states of mental illness. Early psychometrics used infancy in the classification of idiots. An adult with a *mental age* of under three was accordingly clas-sified as an idiot (mental age between three and seven meant *imbeciles*, between seven and ten *morons*). The intelligent quotient was obtained by dividing the mental age by the actual age and multiplying it by a hun-dred. A forty-year-old with a mental age of two would therefore have an intelligence quotient of 5. John Locke often mentioned "Ideots" in the same breath as "Children" when describing reflective inability, for ex-ample. William E. Suter's adaptation of a play by Eugène Grangé en-titled *The Idiot of the Mountain* (1862) contains a scene in which the village idiot, Claude Marcel, is taken in tow by a group of children and storms round the corner with flowers in his hat, a bouquet in his hand, and an idiotic smile on his lips.

Evert Larock, *Der Idiot (De Onnozele)*, 1892.
The idiot must always be reflected by children.

A little later Nietzsche will portray Jesus as a childish simpleton, for one thing because he lived in his own isolated world ("You feel his inability to understand a reality"), furthermore because he lacked heroic "manliness" (anyone who invites a second blow must be out of his mind), and finally because he was backward from every point of view ("Not the faintest whiff of science, taste, mental discipline, logic has fanned these holy fools"). Jesus would have agreed here, since this is exactly the path that every Christian needs to follow: "Truly I tell you, unless you change and become like little children, you will never enter the kingdom of heaven" (Matt. 18:3). Nietzsche doesn't acknowledge the specific quality of the messianic idiot type, and so all he can see even in Kant's ethics is a "recipe for decadence, even for idiocy." Kant as idiot. The angriest of all philosophers, however, who sees the rise of the superman in a witless shepherd ("No longer shepherd, no longer man - a transfigured being")—as a shallow reflection of pastoral power—forgets that anemia precedes blood production, and naivety innovation. In Nietzsche's self-acted intellectual inertia lingers Moreau's definition of genius, which "does not progress to madness or idiocy, but remains stationary, like a kind of arrested mental illness" (Oskar Panizza)—a "stable genius," so to speak. The cliché of genius and madness, which supposedly overlap but actually follow each other, comes from this time, though it can already be found in Montaigne and extends back to antiquity. In the twentieth century, however, the airy artist genius gadding about beyond madness in happy professional naivety will again be discerned in Picasso's work with young children, for example. Carl Gustav Jung also referred to this aspect in his terse note on Dada: "Too idiotic to be schizophrenic." This frolicking in the felicity of the very first idea also applies outside of art. In Children's Letters to God (1991) Eric Marshall and Stuart Hample quote a young girl, Margo, who writes: "Dear God, my father is very smart, maybe he can help you?" The first realm is abruptly seen in the eye of God because the naivety of the address turns its sincerely attempted veneration into a total strength that sees in the creator of the world a pitiful goon. This is far more merciless than declaring him dead, as Nietzsche did. And because it is uttered by a child it is not only funny but true. It is the gentlest idiocy, which dispatches the absolute with a flyswat.

*Aloneliness*—Idiocy and philosophy also lie close together in the first realm: "Philosophy does not contemplate, reflect, or communicate, although it must create concepts for these actions or passions." (Deleuze & Guattari). Philosophical endeavor is like a shallow confrontation at the lonely beginning of things. Heidegger's hallowed "thinking of the philosophers" is a confrontation of the subjectless subject with the immanence of the idiot, in which the philosophical concepts coexist. The suspicion of idiocy already applies to traditional philosophical paradigms. For what contemporary physicians say about the idiot—that he is alone, sequestered from the rest of nature—describes Descartes's modern subject, which, similarly to Esquirol's patient sitting on a horse without riding away, acts quite independently from context and only needs itself to be sure of itself. And doesn't this isolationism likewise parallel the philosophic way of life? Descartes avers that he comes to his understanding in the seclusion of winter. In 1913 Wittgenstein declares the same from his Norwegian hut. According to Descartes such isolation from the world reflects the hutted existence of God, the perfect and indubitable concept that his existence must necessarily belong to his perfection. The world is everything that is the case, after all. There is no world beyond the case. For in the seclusion of the moment there is nobody else who could be the case. Descartes and Wittgenstein conceive these alonelinesses as "proof" because all thoughts lead to one another without leaving the front room. "The I who came thus | The I who will pass away thus | Is the same I living | In this small hut all alone," echoes the Zen monk Sengai Gibon (1750–1837), invoking an immanent understanding from a spatial and temporal afar. It will turn up in the necessity of "the matter itself"—a Cartesian formulation that will later inspire Edmund Husserl to reconstruct the interior of the "hut." But introspection has paranoid traits from the outset, for Descartes hypostatizes a demon that questions the experience of all reality. The natural light of the "idiosopher" shines out against the obfuscation of the demon and gives birth to the transcendent ego as the hypostasis of an intellectual delusion. The demon is a methodical pretext for illuminating the nexus of thinking and being. Nietzsche finds this spurious: "When there is thought there has to be something 'that thinks' is simply a formulation of our grammatical custom that adds a doer to every deed. [...] If one reduces the proposition to 'There is thinking, therefore there are thoughts,' one has produced a mere tautology: and precisely that which is in question, the 'reality of thought,' is not touched upon." Descartes's demon may manipulate the perceptual world, but language remains strangely untouched by the sabotage. Against this background Gilles Deleuze can describe Descartes's act as idiotic while at the same time relating it to the basic task of philosophy, the question of self and meaning. Doesn't Fredric Jameson also concur in his *Hegel Variations* (2010) when he writes of a "narcissism of the absolute" and reduces Hegel's dialectic to the process of self-consumption, unable to think beyond the self-defined horizon or confront the self with radical difference? What is the idiot other than someone who starts and ends with himself? With Hegel this should be understood both systemically and biographically. As Karl Rosenkranz wrote in 1844 about the student Hegel: "There was nothing particularly sharp about him in those days. His youthful acquaintances in Swabia were astonished by his later fame." And from Rudolf Haym: "His teachers sent him on his way with the reference that he was a man of good facility but moderate industry and knowledge, a poor speaker and a philosophical idiot." Perhaps it was this lack of sharpness that predisposed Hegel to the *Phenomenology of Spirit*, (1807), which is pervaded not by a crystalline but a dully thrusting language that is perfect for keeping the motor of dialectic, the "bureaucracy" of absolute reason, ticking over. "Playing the fool, that's always been one function of philosophy," notes the Korean-German philosopher Byung-Chul Han. As we see, it's also a function of the idiot to play the philosopher. The idiosopher—the self-sage—senses both sides of the equation.

*Prima philosophia*—Idiot types of the first order are subjects starting out. The American comedian Chris Rock once told of a man holding a hat out in front of him on the street. A passerby asks him what he's doing. The man replies that he's homeless. "But you don't look like a homeless person!?" And the man assures him: "It's my first day." Starting out, you're not how you are when you've been doing it longer. But how are you when you've been doing it longer? Do you feel the beginning in the same way that you feel an end? The idiot of the first order is essentially a beginner—pioneer, firstborn, primate. He never becomes a "real" professional. He turns the existential aspect of being "thrown out" into a "bandying about," and his structural naivety creates new registers of conviction: as a child, for example, I thought that spaceships could only fly at night, because it seemed to me that space wasn't available during the day.

*Tautological*—Clément Rosset writes: "Even superficially, at the outer margin of their existence, [things] are unknowable: not because they are of this kind, but quite simply because they are." Wittgenstein was convinced that children had to be great philosophers in order to understand school arithmetic: "The existential [...] is opposed to the realm of abstract knowledge," says Fredric Jameson. Abstract knowledge, according to Lacan, never accumulates in a concrete subject but is manifested in a structural void to which knowledge is attributed (*le sujet supposé savoir*). For Marx, ideology has the function of reconciling the existential world with the abstract—for example through the operation of primordialism, the idea that everything is so because it has always been so. The idiot of the first order is ranged even before this order, at the beginning that in a sense has no beginning—analogous to Imre Kertesz's "fateless" one, who can talk of the "happiness of the concentration camp," and that "there is nothing impossible that we do not live through naturally." Such are the acts of signification in every experience of a beginning, and every such experience presupposes an expectation of all eventualities. This applies not just to literature and art. It will be very difficult to convince people claiming, for example, to have "psychological problems" that they perhaps have no psyche in the way they like to believe or in the way they "own" these problems. Psyche is reified self-relation. A problem is framed as "psychological" in advance, and thus appears insoluble. Overcoming problems means inventing problem-free circumstances. It means being able to make a new start, and have to invent a new psyche to fit the solution every time. You have to address the beginning of the problem, which doesn't automatically have to mean "childhood." The naive person questions the authority of knowledge, but without arguing "territorially." Naivety isn't without presuppositions, it creates blank slates by nonchalantly bypassing the limits of the "adult" world. This relates to human *initium*, as Hannah Arendt sees it: "It is not the beginning of something but of somebody, who is a beginner himself." Its result is ingenuousness. Naivety presupposes the unimagined, and every attempt to place it at a false beginning misses the heart of the new and thus the reach of the first realm of the idiot. Isn't this where the claim of all politics originates, as instanced by Paolo Virno: in the "generically human experience of beginning something again, an intimate relationship with contingency and the unforeseen, being in the presence of others"?

*Simplification*—Everyday rationality encompasses complex structures; euphoria only understands "high simplicity." This is why clumsy sloganeering is often the result of failure to attain this simplicity without trivializing the complexity of a situation. Here lies the classical problem of mediation. In his *Thoughts on the Interpretation of Nature* (1754) Denis Diderot faces the question of whether the natural world would be more understandable to us if God had explained it outright in a book. The question is handled as *Bonini's paradox* today, whereby the complete explanation of a complex system will become as complex as the system itself and therefore ineffectual as an explanation. Paul Valéry abbreviates such deliberations to "Everything simple is false. Everything complex is unusable"—a simple explanation that for once seems to be true. Either we describe circumstances truthfully, without getting anywhere, or we deceive ourselves briefly, without getting anywhere. The tendency of non-naive simplification doesn't just lie in media practice but is already founded in post-political "mediality," that is, the absorption of the beginning into the realm of experience. This can be seen today, for example, in the political communication of complex political processes through simple patterns: us/them, pro-life/pro-choice, closed borders/open borders.

*Witless fancies*—The idiot of the first order isn't concerned with having generally no idea, but with having no idea in the right way. "Important scientific discoveries were almost always made by outsiders, or by scientists with unusual careers. Einstein, Bohr, Born were 'dilettanti,' and called themselves so," writes Paul Feyerabend. This has to do with the establishment of knowledge through "an institutional power game played jointly by amateurs and 'true scientists,'" as German literary scholar Uwe Wirth notes. The idiot of the first order is the cause of intellectual incidents here. He reminds the professional generators of knowledge of their original mission. Kant calls the "beginning of thought" that the idiot articulates a "lucky chance" of reason. But the idiot also serves as the catalyst of unreason in his erratic reformulation of knowledge to open up impossible spheres of thought: "A kind of madman, [...] who discovers in thought an inability to think" (Deleuze & Guattari). He functions as "anti-philosopher" and draws attention to the subversive function of thought. Ultimately he shows that even a free society needs to be liberated.

*Second realm*—The idiot of the first order moves flexibly between studio, kindergarten, and padded cell. He descends from the heights of thought to the depths of unreason, ascends to the pinnacle of unreason and ends up at the demise of language and thought——in the second realm, which contains the figure of the idiot as the embodiment of inefficiency, dysfunction, or self-destruction. As system failure, performative contradiction, narcissistic malfunction, auto-aggression, as "destruction as cause of becoming" (Sabina Spielrein), as death drive. As a *strategos* cultivating Voltaire's garden. As a biblical masochism of *cupio dissolvi*, the longing for self-elimination, "a desire to depart and to be with Christ; which is far better" (Phil. 1:23). "Idiotic!" is the last word. Not the beginning but the end seen from its beginning. The second realm relates to the individual idiot, like the first Chinese emperor, Qin Shi Huang, who took mercury pastilles for eternal life and died from them. It also relates to the many idiots: "It is hard to find words," writes Noam Chomsky, "to capture the fact that humans are facing the most important question in their history—whether organized human life will survive in anything like the form we know—and are answering it by accelerating the race to disaster." Why this is so is elucidated, but perhaps not quite explained, by an "anatomy of human destructiveness" as Erich Fromm described it. In the 1960s Günther Anders spoke of a basic human "apocalypse blindness" to describe the consequences of "Herostratic consciousness." Herostratus was an ancient arsonist who wanted to attain eternal fame by burning down the Temple of Artemis, but ultimately fell victim to *damnatio memoriae* (perhaps not quite so, since he is mentioned here). In the ethical wide shot the human tendency to self-sabotage looks like the mystical victory of an absurd Thanatos over Eros, short-circuiting interest with indifference without a motive. A gigantic WHY is answered by an even more gigantic BECAUSE.

*Negative investment*—Robert Musil once described the sinking Danubian Monarchy as "Kakania," giving a name to the flooded bulkhead before the gates of Arcadia. From the perspective of Georges Bataille's "solar economy," self-sabotage means that excess energy created by every living individual is invested in the demise of this life. Downfall is an endeavor that pays off, from the idiot's point of view. Gustav Metzger's *Auto-Destructive Art Manifesto* (1960) similarly marvels at "the obsession with destruction, the pummeling to which individuals and masses are subjected [...], the co-existence of surplus and starvation; the increasing stock-piling of nuclear weapons – more than enough to destroy technological societies; the disintegrative effect of machinery and of life in vast built-up areas on the person." And this still applies, to the same extent that it did during the nuclear-conscious era of the Cold War. This second realm—ranging from conflict to disaster to apocalypse—covers the unexplainable, the annoying, the recalcitrant, which are generally called idiotic today but not explained medically. The happy prophets of economic potential and social progress—from Robert Shiller to Steven Pinker—avoid the dystopian liaison of capital, corruption, and climate, those most reliable indicators of what is to come. Despite the benefits of civilization—worldwide decline in child mortality and illiteracy—there seem to be mercury-eaters and arsonists lurking around every corner. In the Middle Ages the ship of fools was still known as a symbol of metaphysical defiance, but there was still a helmsman Christ in the symbol of the fish who could steer one towards salvation. In contrast, modernity has brought us *Moby Dick* (1851) or JAWS (1975) as fitting maritime metaphors.

*Dark dialectic*—The second realm of the idiot sabotages our basic expectation of a good and happy life. Much would be easier without idiotic dysfunctions and the spanners that can be thrown into the works of existence. The world would be at peace, conflicts solved rationally, accidents avoided through forethought; relationships would be harmonious, bureaucracy humane and efficient, the economy beneficial to society, which would be classless, the state apparatus would voluntarily "wither away." This wellness world immediately dissolves in its own complacency, for isn't there also something inherently idiotic about the trouble-free progression and the fulfilled ideal? Doesn't the scheming Iago necessarily emerge from Othello's realm, which he senselessly but purposefully plunges into ruin? What force apart from gravity pulls us downward? Isn't the schemer also part of a preordained cycle, a cosmic "family constellation"? Aren't perfect harmony, complete satisfaction, and great good fortune doomed in the gardens of Arcadia because they imply nothing but themselves? Even the "concrete utopia" (Ernst Bloch) needs concretion. However, aren't the concretions of an emancipated species-being also subject to "dark" dialectic with continuing effects beyond class and capital? "What if we abandon this utopian notion of Communism and admit that there will be tensions and antagonisms also in Communism, just tensions and antagonisms of a different order that we cannot even properly imagine today?" asks Slavoj

Žižek. How liberal is an unconstrained society? Isn't the tediousness of the good an impetus for evil? The reason why villains are more interesting than heroes lies in the fact that villains get to the heart of things without being interested in this heart. So doesn't even the most perfect future society call for a state beyond its own good fortune, for the sake of preserving the equilibrium of a still unknown social mysticism? "Where in this brave new world are the wastrels, the bums, troublemakers, crooks, and grumblers" wondered the German intellectual troublemaker Wolfgang Pohrt. What does it mean to subject oneself to dark dialectic? Isn't the entirely unnecessary perversely necessary in this second realm? Isn't the self-saboteur an indispensable phenomenon here? The idiot that we desperately need? Not an evolutionary aberration, but the embodiment of the idiotic nature of the social? Not beyond but this side of good and evil? What would be left of life if we got what we desired? Not even boredom. Fernando Pessoa noted in his *Book of Disquiet* (1929–34): "But if I had the kings of my dreams, what would I have left to dream? If I had impossible landscapes, what other impossibilities would remain for me to imagine?" Perhaps the configuration of the second realm is the timeless expression of a fundamental imbalance between fulfilment and expectation, of an "unhappy consciousness," to cite Hegel, gone astray between losing and gaining the world? There is a part of aspiration that turns against itself, because the fulfilment of a goal also represents a threat. An article in the online *Conversation* titled "The Five Biggest Threats to Human Existence" (2014) lists these as nuclear conflict, bioengineering, superintelligence, nanotechnology, unknown unknowns. Happiness is never mentioned as a danger. Following Günther Anders, we don't need Herostratus to discern the second realm of the idiot. Herostratic consciousness is also realized in future world peace, which has rid itself of the bomb in order to look for new disasters.

*Fulfilled contradiction*—Idiocy of the second order shoots an arrow around the world to strike down the archer, thus bringing home what would have become clear anyway ("the world is round"), but not in such a self-sabotaging—idiotic—way. How else can we describe the case of the American student organization White Women Against Racism, which rejected an Afro-American woman's application for membership on the grounds that whites could only talk among themselves about why they excluded Blacks? When "critical whiteness" culminates in an act of exclusion, it compares with self-referential setups like the *Useless Machine*, conceived by Marvin Minsky and developed by his teacher Claude Shannon in 1952, which switches itself off as soon as it is turned on. This apparatus—which can also be read as an ideological mechanism—is typically idiotic: it functions through turning against its single function. Think of computer updates, or service personnel supposed to accomplish one task to improve our lives but creating misery in doing so. The idiotic machine of the second order is a practical tautology, as it always functions even when it doesn't, and vice versa. There are performative contradictions throughout the second realm. A few years ago fighters of the Al-Nusra Front involved in the Syrian civil war drew attention to themselves by abducting forty UN soldiers in order to assert one of their main demands: to be deleted from the United Nations list of terrorists.

*Cold idiocy*—The medical term "cold idiocy" perhaps describes self-sabotage most aptly. This is the phenomenon of freezing people tearing their clothes off and thus freezing more quickly. Some frozen people are found naked, which sometimes has the appearance of an act of violence. There are few explanations: sluggish blood circulation may lead to a subjective sense of heat that causes the freezing person to misjudge the situation and act "idiotically." This can be interpreted as an evolutionary mechanism to accelerate an inevitable death, but when is death inevitable? In some cases the victims crawl under ledges or benches in the final stages and die in a cowering position. It is not known why.

*Hot idiocy*—Idiocy doesn't just prevail over the single organism; it also influences the body of the political economy. It's in accord with the inner contradictions of modern capitalist society. Karl Marx emphasizes the rational basic structure of this self-sabotage in his description of the "idiocy of the present-day bourgeois world": "That anything can ultimately destroy its own cause is a logical absurdity only for the usurer enamoured of the high interest rate. The greatness of the Romans was the cause of their conquests, and their conquests destroyed their greatness. Wealth is the cause of luxury and luxury has a destructive effect on wealth. […] The idiocy of the present-day bourgeois world cannot be better described than by the respect, which the 'logic' of the millionaire […] inspired in all England." The profiteer is the extended arm of the bourgeois subconscious, the avant-gardist of capital whose activity illustrates the aspirations of the bourgeoisie—and these run through the twentieth century unbroken. In 2000, shortly before the dot-com crisis, the German tabloid *Bild* featured the headline "Now We'll All Be Millionaires!" This evergreen "logic of the millionaire," now inflated into that of the billionaire, turns dialectically against itself and "produces, above all, […] its own grave-diggers" (Marx). Keynesians translate this self-sabotage today as market inefficiency. In his bestseller *Irrational Exuberance* (2000), Robert Shiller refers to the bizarre optimism with which market players take on risks and precipitate their downfall while posing as winners. From Shiller's perspective the bubble of the new economy around the turn of the millennium and the global financial crisis of 2008 resulted from an irrational enthusiasm manifested by the hypertrophic consciousness of the global markets. Countless photographs of office men and women with outstretched arms circulate the worldwide web as symbols of success. Everything points upwards: arrows, eyes, arms, balance sheets. It is the semiotic equivalent of the freezing person—a kind of "hot idiocy." Success in the final stages blanks out all incompetence. Nietzsche notes: "No victor believes in chance." And the midday sun casts no shadow.

*Economy of death*—Production and destruction, war and economy become equivalent at the endorphin level. Consumerist slogans have always urged us to keep up the pace ("While stocks last!"). Seen in the light of the second realm, the apocalypse is always trivial and mundane: if no one buys anything, we all perish, and if all we do is buy, we also perish. If we all withdraw our money from the banks, the economy breaks down (bank run). We perish if we all do the same thing, and we perish if we don't. The question is, how and when. From the perspective of the second realm, the rumbling of the end is subsumed into today's promise of good fortune. Once the secret obvious to everyone is revealed, it shows "the dead man, turned to dust by the desiccated economy; an order poor in worldliness that traffics in bodies and life" (Achille Mbembe). In the 1970s the French Marxist Jacques Camatte reduced this diagnosis to a necro-economic formula: "Capitalist society is death organized with all the appearances of life. [...] The human being is dead and is no more than a ritual of capital." Marlon Brando improvised this—more or less at the same time—on the set of APOCALYPSE NOW (1979). The "horror" that Colonel Kurtz is murmuring about is something of which he is a symptom, and this is why he yearns for his ritual killing, why he wants to take the conditions of production down with him and end the cycle of economy-death. Contemporary blueprints of the future, whether their focus is economic, ethical, or technological, correspondingly delineate an *economy of life* with the primary task, as Achille Mbembe writes, of laying down "reserves of life."

*A slender thread*—To summarize: the idiot stands in the public eye, in his first realm as the mystery of beginning, of art, as childlike mania, as inherent Schweikian executive, on the second as symptom of inner contradiction, blind destruction, or metaphysical disorientation, as found in the image of the Medieval sinking ship of fools. The two realms can be kept apart analytically, but experience shows that they merge, overlap, or fluctuate: "And yet a slender thread links the two idiots, as if the first had to lose reason so that the second rediscovers what the other, in winning it, had lost in advance" (Deleuze & Guattari). The relationship is more complex than the image of the thread implies. The idiot links society, thought, and history in the same way as he undoes them.

# THE CRUDEST PATTERN

*Gentlemen, gentlemen, don't think so much!*
Anton Chekhov, *A Happy Man*

*Collateral campaign*—In *The Man Without Qualities* Robert Musil writes: "Another point about idiots is that in the basic concreteness of their thinking they have something that is generally agreed to appeal to the emotions in a mysterious way; and poets appeal directly to the emotions in very much the same way, insofar as their minds run to palpable realities. And so, when Friedel Feuermaul addressed Meseritscher as a poet, he could just as well—that is, out of the same obscure, hovering feeling, which, in his case, was also tantamount to a sudden illumination—have called him an idiot, in a way that would have had considerable significance for all mankind." Having spoken of the lowliest of figures, an idiot, in the next breath he brings its humanity to light. Brackets are placed around the shared foundation of poets and idiots. What is it that they share? Musil: "For the element common to both is a mental condition that cannot be spanned by far-reaching concepts, or refined by distinctions and abstractions, a mental state of the crudest pattern, expressed most clearly in the way it limits itself to the simplest of coordinating conjunctions, [...] and it may be said that our world, regardless of all its intellectual riches, is in a mental condition akin to idiocy; indeed, there is no avoiding this conclusion if one tries to grasp as a totality what is going on in the world." Understanding the totality means conceiving the idiot as a "collateral campaign" of art and society, as Musil perhaps would put it. Thought has mistrusted the thoughtless masses since Plato. Musil, however, seems to be saying that we shouldn't generalize this resentment, as the more the thinker isolates himself from the masses, the more abstract and unnerving he appears to them. At some point intellectual pride topples into the horde from which it thought itself free. Versifying without risk says nothing that hasn't already been said. Distance from the masses can collapse at any moment, and with Musil it's even the precondition for poetry. "Connectedness revitalizes in isolation," writes Botho Strauß. Musil's "crudest pattern" means starting at the bottom if you want to understand how things and beings are related. When he writes of imbecility, he means the foundations of the world liberated from the veil of complexity, and to which the ordinary idiots (simpletons) and extraordinary idiots (poets) have access. So Nicholas's spoon-carver is not only an intelligent nerd but also a member of the dull community of pilgrims who blindly pursue a goal that is even approved by ecclesiastical authority. And they would pursue this goal to their doom.

*Brackets*—Musil's crudest pattern refers to the ubiquity of the concept of idiocy, which Clément Rosset also emphasizes: "One has to take the word in all its meanings: stupid, gratuitous, like the infinity of the possible, but also simple, unique, like the totality of the real itself." The "infinity of the possible" and the "totality of the real" are idiotic because they presuppose nothing but themselves. It's difficult to bracket together two infinities epistemologically: on the one hand the transcendence of all possible forms (possibility exceeds reality); on the other the immanence of the real (the totality of experience is complete, but indeterminate). Yet the approach is important, in order to underline the ontological relevance of the idiot, which goes beyond metaphor, psychiatry, and culture, even though it is dealt with in these spheres. As Dürrenmatt once observed, nothing can fall out of reality. Yes, but you have to open the bracket first, which brings everything together at the level of the crudest pattern.

*The family idiot*—Gustave Flaubert, perhaps like no other writer, and above all as the author of the *Dictionary of Received Ideas*, stands for the "mental state of the crudest pattern." Anecdotes like the ones contemporary neurologists tell of their patients are related about the backward innocent Gustave, whom Jean-Paul Sartre labeled the "family idiot": Gustave takes expressions literally and doesn't understand the meta-level; he "believes everything he is told, out of awe before the verbal object" (Sartre); he has "a poor relationship with words," and is unable to express himself adequately; dialogues aren't a matter of reciprocity for him, but occur in alternating monologues; he only accepts feelings as his own if they are reflected and permitted by authorities, and in general he can only express passions in their rawest form and can't influence his surroundings otherwise; his gestures don't match his emotions; he can't make his own decisions, still can't read at the age of seven, is "stupid, credulous, backward," and so on. According to Sartre this enables Flaubert to apprehend events at the lowest level of their occurrence. And language seems to him to be the first available tool, along with being a symptom of his idiocy. For Flaubert "confuses sign and meaning to the extent that the material presence of the sign is the evidence that guarantees the truth of the meaning," and he views language as an autonomous art of the pharynx. This constellation gives rise to the modern "disinterested" novel, which explains the absence of the author with its realism, and to the most important novelist of the nineteenth century, a "martyr to style" (Walter Pater). It isn't that an idiot becomes a genius here, but rather that the outer idiot "brings out" the inner idiot, and this bringing-out is recognized and accepted as an artistic achievement by the contemporary bourgeois intellectual milieu. Yet from the idiot's point of view writing is a compulsive accomplishment, a neurotic practice for which there is no alternative or explanation.

*Thompsonization*—But there is that other thing that can be expressed in one word. Still under the impression of the war and the events of the Paris Commune, Flaubert writes to George Sand in 1871: "The masses [...] are always idiotic," as they are mere quantity, which overrides the qualities of the individual in the nameless collective. So says Flaubert the bourgeois. Gustave the idiot, however, would long since have understood that the idiocy of the masses had rubbed off onto the writer, that he was cultivating evidence of affinity through disassociation. In 1850, during his journey through Egypt, Gustave gives an account of the vandalism of a wealthy business man: "In Alexandria, a certain Thompson, from Sunderland, wrote his name in letters six feet high on Pompey's column. It can be read a quarter of a mile off. There is no way of seeing the column without seeing the name of Thompson. This imbecile has become part of the monument and is perpetuated with it. What can I say? He crushes it by the splendor of his gigantic letters. Isn't it very clever to force future travelers to think of you and remember you?" Gustave is fascinated by the audacity with which the business man distinguishes himself more clearly from the masses than a writer would ever be able to do. Thompson is a common name, but in his deed all those who don't write their names on columns have become part of the "idiotic" masses. This audacity impresses Gustave, who "from one end of his life to the other, [...] regarded himself as an inessential accident" (Sartre). Doesn't his "active passivity," continually noted by Sartre, also explain his fascination with the imbecile, who makes such an impact that his act can be observed from afar and not just from the pages of a book? In the same year Flaubert begins work on *Madame Bovary*. The novel will be met with the outrage the author found dormant in himself when confronted with the vandalized Egyptian pillar. In other words, Flaubert operates on *the level of the crudest pattern*, and a Thompson appears before him as suddenly as his epileptic fits occur. On the same level—to mention a contemporary—the mad Nietzsche intervenes in Raskolnikov's dream scene of an old horse being mishandled by a carriage driver. It is one of the synchronicities of world literature that Nietzsche departs from sanity to the *idios kosmos* with a Dostoyevskian "reenactment" in 1889. Only seven years later a groundbreaking character will emerge from the same cosmos to elevate Thompsonization into an artform.

*Active simplicity*—In the first edition of the magazine *Acéphale* in 1936, Georges Bataille wrote that "the time of reason and culture is past." The moment they departed can be dated precisely to the evening of December 9, 1896, in the Théâtre de l'Œuvre, when a little turnip-shaped man stumbled onto the stage and exclaimed "merdre!" It was the opening of Alfred Jarry's farce *Ubu Roi*, the story of an infantile tyrant's rise to power. Having arrived in the world, the newly crowned King Ubu decerebrated it, revealing the level of the crudest pattern, which William Butler Yeats, who was at the premiere of *Ubu*, paraphrased as the rise of a "barbarian god." It isn't hard to follow this rise through the twentieth century: "Since 1896 the savage gods have caused the wholesale destruction of the world [...], a destruction more comprehensive and a million times more horrific than Ubu's nightmares" (Claude Schumacher). The history of the crudest pattern is the history of the avant-gardes, and this is the history of microscopic revolutions. Ubu is its first modern fulfilment. The Dada movement was its second: "What we need, what offers some interest, what is rare because it has the anomalies of a precious being and the freshness and freedom of great antimen, is the IDIOT" wrote Tristan Tzara. The Dadaists, as worthy successors to King Ubu, advocated the rebirth of the idiot from the spirit of an incoherent world. "We are often told that we are incoherent [...]. Everything is incoherent. The gentleman who decides to take a bath but goes to the movies instead. The one who wants to be quiet but says things that haven't even entered his head. [...] There is no logic. Only relative necessities [...] The acts of life have no beginning or end. Everything happens in a completely idiotic way" (Tzara). For this reason the Dada Manifesto of 1918 calibrates everything to the crudest pattern, which demands the zero metaphor of the savior, and so Dada works "with all its might towards the universal installation of the idiot" (Tzara). This isn't a discrete practice but a dialectic of the idiot that is constantly played out. The Dada Manifesto of 1918 delineates the art-savior Dada as the synthesis of two idiot types:

> *Thesis:* "The love of novelty is the cross of sympathy, demonstrates a naive je m'enfoutisme, it is a transitory, positive sign without a cause." (*Idiot type of the first order*)

*Antithesis:* "I say: there is no beginning and we are not trembling. we are not sentimental. We shred the linen of clouds and prayers like a furious wind, preparing the great spectacle of disaster, fire, decomposition." (*Idiot type of the second order*)

*Synthesis:* "Active Simplicity." (*"State of the crudest pattern"* = *Dada*)

The precept of active simplicity can be followed into contemporary art production, for example to Fischli & Weiss and their manifesto-like instructions for action, which end in the prosaic injunction to smile. Alfred Jarry's pataphysical practice of decerebration reminds us to look in two directions like Janus: the wide-angled vision of the new is also that of the person on the way out. But simultaneously it holds that at no time is everything lost, because this "everything" doesn't exist. "Everything" is the flow in which everything is.

*Situation*—Following the Dadaists, the *dérives*, *détournements*, and "constructed situations" of the situationists represent fluid attempts at the crudest pattern before it had an art label. On New Year's Eve of 1953 Guy Debord, Gilles Ivain, and Gaetan Langlais—all around twenty—go on a bar hop during which they run riot and provoke guests until Debord has to terminate the action in a drunken stupor. So you're only loud enough when you write, not when you shout. The strategic disorientation of the situationists, "its paradoxical blend of the concreteness of the political manifesto with a poetic elusiveness" (Tom McDonough), forms the central paradox of their "nihilist romanticism" (Claire Bishop), namely that the "abolition and realization of art are inseparable aspects of a single *transcendence of art*" (Debord). Their three-fold intensity—artistic avant-garde, everyday experimentation, social revolution—is intended to overcome the society of spectacle on the level of the crudest pattern, without adopting the stance of rational argumentation. The *détournement* was meant as something essentially primitive, an irrational subversion whose political ends weren't always clear. It is represented by the "constructed situation," which can be traced back to Henri Lefebvre's theory of moments, the creation of a collectively organized practice that leads to a "game of events" (Bishop), "producing ourselves, and not things that enslave us." As described by Raoul Vaneigem in his *Traité* (1967), every act of frenzy creates the possibility of an "intuitively 'radical' proletariat engaged in spontaneous activity" (David Jacobs) and unlocks the power of the disorientated, "because [their] drunkenness is continual and its resulting farsightedness therefore knows no interruption, not a single 'sober' phase can disturb [their] apathy" (Rosset). This permanent state, according to Vaneigem, corresponds to the ethos of a "new innocence": "[Revolutionary] tactics entail a certain kind of hedonistic foresight. [...] We have a world of pleasures to win, and nothing to lose but boredom."

*The idiocy of health*—Seen from the plane of consistency, or the "planomenon," as coined by Deleuze & Guattari, all acts are intensities that are unrepresentable, insubstantial, and in a certain sense "pure." The zero expression, the crudest pattern, active simplicity, the constructed situation, and so on, are paradoxical representations of something unrepresentable—or, shall we say, nothing but "a tale | Told by an idiot, full of sound and fury, | Signifying nothing." Hence arises the question of whether the idiotic act is art or politics or something else. And it's this "something else" that needs looking at. Thompson's lone vandalism carries over the principle of the many to the principle of the one through the blunt force of representation. In this way the name is hustled onto the building, the message onto the stone tablets, the imagination into the book, the brand onto the market. Leave your own mark: self-branding is practiced today by business people, artists, politicians, and tourists immortalizing themselves on monuments—"You've got to put your name on stuff or no one remembers you," said Donald Trump about George Washington's failure to exploit his historical brand name more effectively. Idiots are like human formulas, and they function very well. "There are so many of them," writes Flaubert, "they return so often, they are in such good health." If paranoia is an illness of power, as

Elias Canetti claims, then idiocy is the pathology of its health.

*New acts*—In the twentieth and twenty-first centuries the level of the crudest pattern becomes the arena for social debates that attempt to grasp the subliminal with the principles of cultural, social, or political organization. In order to describe the Thompsonization of the world revealed by these debates, the German Fluxus performer and philosopher Bazon Brock coined the term "perpetrator type" (*Tätertyp*) for those whose existential drive is the assertion of their own ideas at any price. In the meantime we have become aware that the realms of the idiot increasingly overlap on the level of intensity, that great ideas always contain their narrowest extent. But some contemporary art both acts out the perpetrator type and overrides it—a meta-Thompsonization on the level of the crudest pattern.

*Minou*

The digital montage *Minou* (2000), by Wim Delvoye, illustrates the possibilities of the signifier that marks the *idion* for coming generations. The promise of permanency can ultimately only be given by the earth—the stone—itself, also including tweets. A comparison with Santiago Sierra's gigantic SOS sign near the Smara refugee camp in Algeria makes the conceptual difference clear. In 2012 Sierra had the graffiti—all eight-and-a-half square kilometers of it—dug into the desert sand by earthmovers in order to draw attention to the Moroccan occupation of Western Sahara (this "largest graffiti in the world" can be seen from space, and was photographed by the satellite Ikonos 3). Both works make use of gigantism to emphasize local phenomena. The first deals with a consumerist sentiment making itself comfortable in an idiotic media abode. In the second the artist uses an "earth sign" surpassing the usual forms of communication to express a political grievance. Both works are "political," though they oppose contemporary power and the dynastic principle in different ways: the first is a criticism of late-capitalist hypertrophy, the second of its imperial logic. Operating on the level of the crudest pattern means doing justice to a situation by putting one's own stamp on it. This arena, where both art and non-art are at home (or absent), can be conceived as a zone of peculiarity, a realm of the real; a zone that has to do with the "matter in question," this matter being concrete, particular, but also elusive and without essence. The imbecile world is the world in intensity.

## THE IDIOTIC REAL

*A theory*—Many years ago I saw one of Peter Jackson's early splatter movies in the theater. During the screening I heard raucous laughter from two male splatter nerds sitting behind me. Their laughter was noticeable because nobody else laughed during these filmic moments I didn't even recognize as "moments." These guys didn't laugh in the obviously comical scenes, for example when two zombies taste spoonfuls of each other's brains (which is funny); instead they laughed during fadeouts (which aren't). The two insiders seemed to enjoy the film more on the level of its texture, to consume it like a ripe fruit—or brain—and give a burp here and there. But there may also be an irrational explanation for such behavior. Slavoj Žižek describes a similar experience: "When I saw The Matrix at a local theatre in Slovenia, I had the unique opportunity of sitting close to the ideal spectator of the film – namely, to an idiot. A man in the late 20ies at my right was so immersed in the film that he all the time disturbed other spectators with loud exclamations, like 'My God, wow, so there is no reality!'" And Žižek adds: "I definitely prefer such naive immersion to the pseudo-sophisticated intellectualist readings which project into the film the refined philosophical or psychoanalytic conceptual distinctions." Senseless sense becomes the bizarre echo of everyday events, and the shallow reflex of the idiot impresses the philosopher because it also resonates within him; the inner idiot communicates with the outer. As a counterpart to the emancipating, consciousness-raising, epic theater, idiotic communication only recognizes initial content, but from Žižek's point of view this is just as theoretical as a film discourse that has gone through the academic ritual. The difference between the typical film critic and the film-going idiot isn't that the critic has a theory and the idiot doesn't. It's rather that the idiot burps out his theory and then doesn't make a fuss about it. Like Forrest Gump says: "I know that bein a idiot an all, I ain't sposed to have no philosophy of my own, but maybe it's just because nobody never took the time to talk to me bout it." But this conjecture is the first step to philosophizing, which flares up here as a collaborative task and once necessitated the midwife metaphor from Plato. The idiot's message is simple: philosophizing means someone taking the time to talk to someone else. You might be clear about the procedure and have analyzed an issue thoroughly, but as soon as you get down to the crudest pattern of experience your inner idiot is revealed. Only a *complete idiot* is time-invariant and never latches on to anything—a state of absolute literalness.

*Confidence*—Literalness is a point of access to the imbecility of the world, for when we take words literally, communication loses its most important instrument: figurative language. Everything metaphorical is broken down to a call for realization; impressions are no longer gathered but blithely scratched onto pillars. The result is a discursive tilt: everyday situations reveal something "real"; that is, from the idiot's mouth flows a truth as if it were a realization, and which only needs a touch of under-complexity to come to light. As Clément Rosset has shown, idiotic discourse is closely connected with the discourse of the real, whereby the real indicates an inexplicable, resistant aspect of a situation, something that according to Lacan evades symbolization, an "internally sensed exterior." I would say, something under-complex and basic. Remember Esquirol's patient, who literally gets on a horse without riding anywhere. One difference between the experience of the real and the experience of reality consists in being *in the symbol* instead of dependent on it. That's why there are no representations of reality, only realizations and entrances. What Nassim Nicholas Taleb calls the "skin in the game" can be generalized into semiotic commitment: as a "signifier" I subject myself to the consequences of signification instead of evading them. This commitment also applies to idiocy, which knows no distance between signifier and signified. An idiot—as a singular semiotic operator—has no choice but to be committed because of his obligation to the sign. Someone who *resolves* to give up her profession doesn't give it up. Someone *considering* emigration stays at home. An idiot doesn't resolve or consider anything. What she signals to do she is already doing. And her devotion may transpose to all kinds of activities, as can be seen, for example, with socially devoted solitaries, "weirdos," or "village idiots." In my city of birth, I knew the mentally impaired loner A., who made it a habit to clean the riverbank or to single-handedly direct the traffic at intersections. He had a savant talent for memorizing all birthdays and familial relationships in the neighborhood, and he often strolled around exclaiming "I know why I was born." A., whose mental condition was caused by an injury to his head during the German bombardment of Yugoslavia in the Second World War, was well regarded in his neighborhood. To us kids he was like an universal uncle from outer space. Later he would become famous throughout the city, with poets writing about him and T-shirts circulating with prints of his above favorite sentence. In certain ways these types of individuals can be trusted blindly, because they don't compete with anybody about anything. They are incorruptible, which is the main reason why they are considered idiots; they are unable to be anything other than what they are. But there is a paradox here: we can trust an idiot in idiot terms, but we can't predict what the idiot may or may not do. The question is whether you can trust someone who is categorically unpredictable. If you can, you have grasped something of the idiotic real.

*Overdetermined*—Ordinary situations become idiotic when official instructions are taken literally, as in the case of the man who falls into the water, sinks like a stone, and has to be rescued by a passer-by. Questioned why he didn't try to reach the bank, he replies: "The sign said 'swimming prohibited.'" There is a sense of humor that draws on literalness, keeping its figures stuck to the sign or putting their foot in their mouth. Many schoolboy jokes go like this: "What was the first thing Queen Elizabeth did when she ascended to the throne?" "She sat down." Or "Where was the Declaration of Independence signed?" "At the bottom." And so on. The aim is to outsmart the prevailing language game on the level of the crudest pattern. This plays out somewhere between slapstick, silliness, and speech-act analysis, and one forgets the semiotic commitment it contains because the power of language is so mundane. Otherwise it wouldn't stand to reason, as the late American comedian Mitch Hedberg enlightened us, that "an escalator can never break. It can only become stairs."

*Representativeness*—When we translate something verbally literal into an image we end up with the popular online meme "Are You Drunk?"

The joke is explained on the one hand from the fact that a third, "impossible" level appears inside a two-valued logic, that is, the given answer is creative; on the other hand that the subject supposed to answer this simple question is obviously physically incapable of doing so, and can only carry out the formal act, that of making a cross. Yet the inability to place the cross correctly delivers a more precise answer than would ever occur to the sober framer of the question. The test person is obviously so drunk that they can't carry out the test correctly, just truthfully. Typically for drunks, they wish to deny their inebriation, insisting on making the cross but missing the box. Instead of declaring this a mistake, it can be claimed that it expresses an inadvertent will (because the cross isn't far enough away to pass as a mistake). Put differently, the devisers of the test are revealed as learned idiots by a clueless idiot. If they had the idiotic instinct, the form might have looked like this:

**ARE YOU DRUNK?**
☐ **YES**
  **NO**
      ☐

And here we assume that the drunk (we always take the same test person) doesn't make a vain attempt to hit the displaced box this time. But if they did, the cross would logically have to land just under the other box, that is, correct in the above sense:

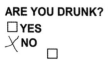

**ARE YOU DRUNK?**
☐ **YES**
✗ **NO** ☐

That would be a minimal definition of genius, or, say, of *perfected unintentionality*. The idiot is always behind or ahead of us, but never "on a par"—and anyway *our* par isn't a binding standard. You could say that this test person is an idiot of the first order who looks like one of the second. A lout who turns out to be a seer precisely because of his realization as a lout. The idiot is someone who indicates—unexpectedly or through true speech—the misconstructions of social life. He breaches the etiquette, infringes the protocol, breaks the decorum, readdresses the fallacious, simplifies to recognition. This is his *idiopractice*. The idiot's anti-communications are surrounded by a pataphysical halo that says "What's all this?"

*Motleycultured*—Scandalous works of art are treated in a similar way, because they are true and because art works with the real, not only with the viewer's expectations. The above imaginary questionnaire therefore recalls Martin Kippenberger's sculpture *Street Lamp for Drunks* (1988), in which the heavy-drinking artist anticipates the curvature of a drunk leaning against a lantern in the lantern itself. A subjective 3D questionnaire, so to speak, with its "boxes" sketched out by the artist. Kippenberger's structural unpredictability visualizes the workings of the real, as Clément Rosset sees it, but not deliriously. Rather, it expresses the sober logic of delirium: haphazard, but definite and necessary; audacious enough to follow its intuition and ignore standards. The idiot's performance is not only immersed in life experience; it can also be understood as an existential formula, as a warning, a gesture, a moronic thing-in-itself, without exhausting itself in the narrow concept of mind. Not superman but supermind and supergod immersed in supernothing. All action is traced back to the level of the crudest pattern, which in turn aspires to the (impossible) experience of the real, in which the imbecility of the world wears motley hues.

*Mystery*—While the real is often discussed in connection with the historical or cultural sublime, the idiot's gesture requires us to profanize the discourse. Confrontation with the real—with Lacan this always has the nimbus of impossibility—shows that there is something that exists in addition to the totality of experience, which can't be ascribed to the symbolic or imaginary. "There is no mystery behind things, but a mystery of things," writes Rosset. This is why the idiot is literal, and why paintings are smarter than their painters, as Gerhard Richter famously claimed, because there is this resistance of the given which reflects the facticity of one's own world. "A fact collides with the idea of doing. It resists because it resists, not yet knowing on which behalf," says Jean-Luc Nancy. The "practical impulse" (Adorno) impels thought without knowledge, and not just what constitutes experience on reflection. The idiot is senseless like sense itself; idiot *per se*, though not in the sense of Kant's theoretical necessity for the *per se*, but beyond correlation and *ex positivo*, becoming with Fichte (and Nietzsche) what he already *is*. The idiot poses the question of what it means to live unboundedly, to cast off all disguises, never having to delude other people, and without resorting to the "tyranny of intimacy" (Richard Sennett). For idiocy isn't about "authentic experience" but rather the impossibility of experience, about the impossibility of thought as its necessity.

*Everything's there*—The idiotic moment gives us a comprehensive answer to the question of the contingent of reality. Jean Dubuffet claims: "Everything that exists is there." Raw reason proclaims the realization of everything. Everything is what the case is: Wittgensteinian Taoism, absolute positivism, total immanentism abbreviated to the sum of all givenness—"What exists belongs completely to the world because it belongs to it *alone*" (Quentin Meillassoux). The idiocy of the concrete is ruled by a priori satisfaction, "active simplicity" (Dada), or the zero expression we know from literary idiots. The imbecilic world is one without transcendence, comparable with fantasy and superhero worlds that have no God because the divine is part of them—worlds "in which there is nothing external that could constrain their power of newness" (Meillassoux). Everything that happens by chance is necessary; there is no transcendence that can ensure the contrast between substance and accident. Furthermore, everything that emerges is measurable, but emergence itself appears not to be—or as Reiner Schürmann notes: "Coming to presence loves to hold itself back." There is always something impossible in everything that is happening, or put differently: we can't grasp the idiotic nature of emergence. If philosophers of mind like David Chalmers reconceptualize consciousness as a fundamental fact of nature due to the "hard problem of consciousness," then perhaps this applies by analogy all the more to the equally nonreducible idiotic. As soon as it emerges, it brings a rationality of the new into the empirical world, exposing the difference between categorical and fundamental impossibility. In a world in which everything is already there, it is *categorically* impossible for anything to happen that is not already "there"—anything new here is "otherworldly" without being transcendent. In a world that is open to transcendence, impossibilities are *fundamental* to the make-up of this world—anything new here transcends the given without being "otherworldly." The idiot's act is impossible *in the categorical sense*, jumping from one immanence to the (impossible) other. Extropy is not a mode of entropy here, and so the new is not a foundational mode of existence—that is, "a newness that before its manifestation was not present in any original principle, nor lying concealed in any demiurgical drawer" (Meillassoux).

*Clarification*—The idiot shows a certain epicurean complacency when confronting serious questions. The ontological difference hasn't yet filtered down to him. He is simply there, without actually "existing," or he exists without actually being "there." And because *everything* is there for the idiot, *everything* is mysterious too. This is why Rosset, referencing Plato—who presupposes an a priori drunken, amorous, or artistic state in the philosophical effort—suggests transcendental ecstasy as an access point to the idiotic real. The permanent ecstasy of thought, of love, the narcissistic immersion, these are the entrances to the real on the level of the crudest pattern which the idiot reveals as sage or saboteur. It helps him to calibrate his senses to a situation, turning like Woody Allen's parade fool Zelig into a human chameleon. Becoming as sluggish and stoned as the political round. Having the look and feel of a building. Becoming under-complex, a hut, a lantern. A revolution, too, is nothing other than the mass living-out of the real on the level of the crudest pattern. In the way that Idiota's pilgrims, narratives, signs, or slogans don't need to be coordinated. Everyone knows what it's about, without actually having to know anything. Collective improvisation—as in jazz—means that everyone is on the inside; you can synchronize, organize, go wild together; nothing needs to be explained or understood. Everyone is drunk without being befuddled. This matches Rosa Luxemburg's idea of political *spontaneity*, according to which revolutionary organization arises from action, and also Hannah Arendt's notion that revolution actualizes human natality: being born so as to act anew, an immanent state of the many in which everyone senses an outside. And although we sense that the seemingly impossible is no ultimate barrier in political matters—despite the ruthless reign of realpolitik—it's still puzzling to us that the impossible is possible at every instant, that circumstances can suddenly reverse. We are surprised by the fact that another world is possible in the next moment, although we know this at birth.

*Indescribable*—Rosset doesn't exemplify the idiotic real as historical dialectic or traumatic experience, as Lacan or Bataille do, but primarily as the mundane experience of singularity: "To say that an object is 'unique' [...] amounts to saying that it exists, that it is real." And it is real because the general determination of reality—its ontological "scheme"—doesn't encompass its idiosyncrasy. Objective descriptions are no use in the attempt to grasp the unique. Rosset mentions a camembert on the table before him that tastes different from all other camemberts. This recalls Henri Bergson's example of the turret clock whose every chime leaves a unique, irreversible impression although all its chimes may objectively be identical (frequency, volume). Time guarantees the non-identical, which can't be apprehended by a descriptive algorithm. The "stain" of a phenomenon, that which makes it unique, can't be compared with other "stains," and can't be both *grasped* and *described*—be it an error, a quirk, an exception in which the real reveals itself. For "The more real an object is, the less it can be identified." And "the more intense the feeling of reality is, the more indescribable and obscure it is" (Rosset).

*Proceeding from itself*—The idiocy of the real presupposes a confrontation that points back to the etymological origin, the Latin and Greek words *objectum* and *problema* ("thing," "object"). Some thing is singular and equal to itself, and suddenly it is confronted with some thing else. A level of encounter is now defined; difference, relationship, and kind are established. Now it is no longer singular and equal to itself, but "one of a kind" [*einzigartig*], in strict relation to the *kind*. Some thing singular and equal to itself has no "problem" and no "objection," only a *property*, from which the problem may result. Here too we must grasp *property* bifocally in the sense of both *feature* and *ownership*. In other words, singular experience can only be had as a problem, only as a confrontation with a property, which, not coincidentally, happens to be the main attribute of Max Stirner's philosophical figure of the "Ego." But it's impossible to speak about all of this with the same directness with which the idiotic proceeds from itself. The basic understanding of the idiot is confronted with the impossibility of projecting or performing anything that goes beyond their singularity. When "we have a situation," when words fail us, when it's clear that it is what it is and no different, then it has come in at "point blank." This moment is the experience of property as a basic form of idiocy: owning something is inherently idiotic—just look at the faces on people when they've bought new stuff. Put differently: property is *indescribable*.

*Descriptive algorithms*—As Pierre Bourdieu has shown, judgments of taste are bound to the different aesthetics of the class society; that is, property is describable in all respects here. But material conditions have become "liquid." Today's class struggle ranges from migrant influx to the inner cities to Internet browsers. Sound out the media echo chamber, and it becomes clear that one's opinion is as describable as one's income. Plentiful descriptive algorithms are at work here, all calibrated to the steady rhythm of the social-media giants. Users are exposed to what the programmers consider to have positive neurotransmitter effects and what influences buying behavior. The streaming giant Netflix, for example, divides its customers into thousands of taste groups so as to personalize its choice of products. Since every choice takes about two seconds, the image algorithms need to be permanently updated according to user behavior. This is done by analyzing viewing patterns enhanced by neuro-optimized networks. On the level of the crudest pattern the *idion* counters with subjects who evade algorithm formation and ultimately their own monetization. If a business model can be made out of virtually anything, the first realm of the idiot represents the forbidden zone of capitalism, the heterogeneousness that can't be commodified or appropriated, standing at the beginning of value creation. There is no adequate formula for a zero expression. The second realm, however, represents the never-ending end of creation. Experience based on descriptive algorithms can only be deciphered, not understood. Experience of the beginning can't be deciphered but *only* understood, in as much as it is unique, a zero. There are no gages for the singular, because the singular creates gages of its own uniqueness. This is why Lacan calls the real the *impossible*, because it can't be invalidated. No terror, no tyranny, no sedation can pervert the inner logic of the subject. We are above all idiotic before we are so free that our freedom can't be taken away. But at the same time being idiotic makes us blind to this very freedom.

*Totality and fragment*—In the eyes of the idiot the entire universe amounts to nothing more than an incomplete gesture: "The idiot speaks only in idioms, though these function for him not as colorful additions to a language or culture, but are understood by him alone" (Eric Anthamatten). The idiot uses a language of fragments, as does Benjy Compson in Faulkner's *The Sound and The Fury* (1929). Benjy is mute, but the first chapter is told from his point of view. The narrative is disjointed, jumping between past and present, conveying trauma as if it were still occurring. Forrest Gump springs similarly from time to space, stuttering himself into the idiot hero of his times, running and running until something holds him up. But all these life fragments claim a totality: "For example, if we say that a conceptual persona stammers, it is no longer a type who stammers in a particular language but a thinker who makes the whole of language stammer" (Deleuze & Guattari). You could say that an idiot doesn't utter words but "secretes" them. They fall from his mouth like hair from his head. And you could say that the environment speaks with the aid of the idiot, in that the idiot passes on all events unfiltered. Benjy is highly sensitive. He smells his sister's loss of virginity ("Caddy smelled like trees in the rain"), and he senses Quentin's suicide from a great distance. Imagination infects its authors. Faulkner describes writing from Benjy's perspective as a unique literary experience of "the emotion definite and physical and yet nebulous to describe which the writing of Benjy's section of *The Sound and The Fury* gave me—that ecstasy, that eager and joyous faith and anticipation of surprise," which would never reoccur.

*Dramaturgies of things*—The idiocy of the real is multifaceted, often expressed in what Jean Arp calls the "magic of chance." In chance events a structure of meaning becomes evident, and it's clear that they obey laws like the determined form of meaning. As Rosset emphasizes, "the manifestations of chance can only occur as far as they are also specific and necessary manifestations." But according to Arp, not everyone has the magical power of being able to recognize the necessary in the co-incident; only dreamers, mystics, or ecstatics know how to access the real. C.G. Jung called this spontaneous calibration of time and meaning "synchronicity," though it is important not to assume a parapsychological transcendence or "higher sphere." Chance events, that is, events that yield meaning in coincidence, are common to all occurrence and yet have something idiotic about them: the idiot asks "Why do the traffic lights always jump to red when I'm in a hurry?" as if the fabric of time had turned against them and they were the most important subjects in the universe to have the privilege of matter personally rebelling against them. Chance events occur outside the redundancy of time patterns or statistical random distribution. What Friedrich Schiller celebrates as the "wind of chance" and Bob Dylan two hundred years later as an "idiot wind" is a chaosmic current that determines human relations and that may be productively used to navigate these relations. Poseidippus once asked Kairos, "Why do you have wings on your feet?" And Kairos answered, "So I can fly like the wind." In his autobiography, *My Last Sigh* (1983), Luis Buñuel remembers a game of chance he played with friends. There is a group of people in a room. One person goes out. Someone moves an object. The person comes back in and has to say which object has been moved and who did it. In this game the solution isn't found through some kind of mentalist cold reading, but through knowing it or even predicting it "by chance," like an idiot would. Even though we continually have to do with the "idiotic nature of improbability" (Bernard Stiegler), and every game of chance is absurd, winged feet have been built into today's economic ratio. For brands too shouldn't be rationally derived but should seem *objective*, as if they had exactly predicted the customer requirement the very second it arose. Customers will buy anything if they feel personally addressed by the entire universe—the fabric of all there is—at any given moment. Every so-called trend-casting operates in a kind of clairvoyant mode. This is paradigmatically embodied in William Gibson's novel *Pattern Recognition* (2003) by the protagonist Cayce Pollard. This is someone who can sense the future or comprehend entire situations *without knowing how*. She is a *cool-hunter*, that is, constantly on the lookout for future trends and new profit generators. "Cayce Pollard [...] is distinguished above all by a capacity to detect the new, to see it coming before everybody else. [...] the reverberations of her own body tell her whether a proposed new way of branding products will work" (Nikolas Kompridis). Like a mixture of physiological detector and a techno-capitalist version of Socrates, she moves in time with agility and uses the contingent as an epistemological and political vehicle. On the one hand there is "the potential power of marketing to create a desire for products that do not exist, and may never exist. In other words, the power to create a consuming desire for what is unconsumable – the mere possibility of newness itself"; on the other hand Pollard hopes "the hope that an openness to the genuinely new will be transformative and redemptive – the hope (or faith) that our possibilities are not exhausted, that a new beginning is still possible; that there is a kind of new that is not commodifiable, that can't be instrumentalized, but rather, answers real human needs." Thus Pollard embodies a new type of political hope that is immunized against the instrumentalization of the new. She contains what Hannah Arendt once called a "mental organ for the future."

*Pure act*—The choreography of chance is a neglected level of political rationality. In *What Is To Be Done?* (2014) Jean-Luc Nancy writes: "Not knowing what to do, not even knowing what one could do without even 'preferring not to,' is to await or interrogate the very possibility of a *doing*, about which one has an idea without having experienced its efficacy." With the idiot it is the reverse: he puts into effect without having a sense of doing, acting out another "inner" doing that parallels the "outer" action, as with von Trier's idiots. As with Faulkner's Benjy, his doing has no signature in time; it is an analogy to the totality of a photon, whose formation and decay are a single quantum event. Someone without a proper mass has no curriculum vitae, only a punctum vitae. Idiotic doing, in this sense, is *pure doing*. Pure acts are those that take place without premise or consequence, that act themselves out in/ with the idiot; that are peculiar to all singular beings, immune against instrumentalization, yet that can also be blank instruments of power; that "can't be 'placed' [...] in existing logical space" (Kompridis); that generate "the new in its pure, uncontaminated form." Pure acts insist. They play out in essence what Schelling describes as the mode of the absolute, before any divine or worldly presentation: *actus purus*, the idiotic ur-principle of doing everything and nothing at once. From the political point of view the blank slate of what is to be done, both creatively and destructively, points to the struggle against the ambivalences of modernity—as Zygmunt Bauman notes, "the feeling of indecision, undecidability, and hence loss of control. The consequences of action become unpredictable, while randomness, allegedly done away with by the structuring effort, seems to make an unsolicited come-back. [...] The struggle against ambivalence is, therefore, both self-destructive and self-propelling."

*Signature*—Everything today is carried away by the endless stream of "liquid modernity" (Bauman), which is becoming apparent as a spectacle of message and image. Everyone who has binge-watched a television series understands instinctively what it means that "goals are nothing, development is everything" (Guy Debord). Development here is future-oriented; it extends the end many times over. Today's spectacle is a social relationship in the flow of self-images reaching from the future to the present. The glut of attempted explanation and ascertainment through big data and social physics is one cause of mental overload from the uncomprehended world. Imagine the madness of being able to know everything about all the bits of information of our own making. Imagine an AI algorithm emulating an autistic person; imagine a savant computer, a computer that cannot be reproduced, a one-of-a-kind thing that does one-of-a-kind things ... Events that evade the spectacular in the midst of the spectacle correspond to real connections within this world. Exceptions aren't exceptions to the rule, they are themselves the rule. The phenomenon of the idiot motivates the attempt by speculative reasoning to break through the conventional understanding of things and beings from two sides: the idiot of the first order evades the spectacular with his deed; the idiot of the second order subjects himself to it entirely.

*Axiomatic action*—"Every reality is necessarily arbitrary, both specific and random, therefore insignificant," writes Rosset. Since no moment is metaphysically distinguished from any other moment, the reality underlying every moment is both definite and random. The operating level of the crudest pattern reverses the instrumental reality of action. The pure act of the idiot is determined by indeterminacy and impossibility, which gives rise to the language game of means and ends. "How oddly everything behaves, | intertwining and then swimming apart: | friendly, somewhat uncertain. | How good," writes Rainer Maria Rilke in the *Song of the Idiot* (1906). An attempt to do something goes against an indeterminacy and impossibility. The incorporation of indeterminacy and impossibility into an attempt operates on the level of the crudest pattern. The idiotic act isn't neutral, as it affects the binarity of meaning, like Blanchot's or Barthes's *neutrum*. A party that attacks two warring parties is both neutral and belligerent. Rational decisions go through the scheme of the idiotic at least once—the excluded third of binarity. How is the indeterminate determined? How is the impossible accomplished? According to Marie Curie it is the dreamers who accomplish the impossible, not the practically disposed. But idiots are practical dreamers who stand for a *bounded reality*—"ordinary, unoriginal, understanding without depth or mystery that you have seized this very moment for living," as the German poet Ludwig Rubiner once put it. There is a "divine" leap into freedom dormant in every ordinariness: the operation is axiomatic, on the level of the crudest pattern, as a phenomenon *before itself.*

# 2
## THE MANY IDIOTS

COMPUTER: Please speak your name as it appears on your current federal identity card …

JOE: I'm not sure if I have an identity card. But my name is …

COMPUTER: You have entered the name "Not Sure." Is this correct, Not Sure?

JOE: What? No! It's not correct!

COMPUTER: Thank you! "Not" is correct! Is "Sure" correct?

JOE: What? No! No, it's not! Go back! Cancel! You've got the wrong name! My name is Joe Bowers! Not "Not Sure."

COMPUTER: You have already confirmed your first name is "Not!" Please confirm your last name, "Sure!"

JOE: No! My last name is not "Sure!" I mean—no, wait!

COMPUTER: Thank you, Not Sure! Your confirmation is complete.

# THE ZEROED SOCIETY

*I'll laugh until my head comes off.*
Radiohead, "Idiotheque"

*Something is different*—To understand what in our present is different from the myriads of presents before it, I place the idiot in political time. If the idiot was an archetypal, cultural, even ontological figure in Part One, now the focus is on why it's relevant *today*. The age of the idiot is initially characterized by an incongruence between the private, particular, singular, on the one hand, and the public, general, universal, on the other. You could also say that it has to do with a learnt inability to apply private, particular, or singular issues to the social whole and vice versa. The condition underlying this mismatch is what I call "idiocracy." This is a state in which social self-sabotage functions as social contract. Idiocracy thus corresponds to the second realm of the idiot. It refers to an "inoperative community" (Nancy) driven by "a consciousness that, under the compulsion of self-preservation, continues to run itself, though run down, in a permanent moral self-denial," as the German philosopher Peter Sloterdijk once described the machinations of cynical reason in late modernity. But thought and action in an idiocracy are driven more by a metaphysical defiance than by a general cynicism. The more talk there is of narcissism, the more narcissism is exactly what we want. The more "weariness of the self" (Alain Ehrenberg), the more frenetically we wear ourselves out. We are constantly warned against the opposite because the opposite is exactly what we want. We want climate death because everyone is warning us about it, and because we ourselves are doing the warning. We want ludicrous strongmen in power because we are repelled by them. We want boundaries because we think ourselves boundless. We want chaos because we love order above all else. We want our downfall because we wallow in growth. We want the antithesis without having to bother about thesis and synthesis. We want the opposite unconditionally.

*The third person*—Idiocracy doesn't need to correspond to a concrete state, just as the literary idiot doesn't need to correspond to a concrete person—but does so nevertheless behind our back, through language, for example, as Deleuze & Guattari explain: "In everyday life speech-acts refer back to psychosocial types who actually attest to a subjacent third person: 'I decree mobilization as President of the Republic,' 'I speak to you as father' [...]. 'I think as Idiot,' 'I will as Zarathustra,' 'I dance as Dionysus,' 'I claim as Lover.' [...] 'Who is "I"?' It is always a third person." Idiocracy refers by analogy to the excluded middle of individual and society. The idiotic defiance of the world is both utopian and dystopian in view of the smoldering zero state, but it doesn't give rise to a proletarian or bourgeois ideal, only to the idiot as society. The embodiment of a question mark. How is the idiocratic Leviathan structured? What policies and mass form does it presume?

*"Not Sure"*—The dystopian comedy IDIOCRACY (2006) plays through the vision of a self-sabotaging society. The soldier Joe and prostitute Rita are recruited for a military research project and put into a deep sleep. Shortly afterwards the research project is abandoned and the sleep pod forgotten ... The two guinea pigs wake up five centuries later in a retarded future. Because of his comparatively high IQ, the former loser Joe, who is registered under the name of Not Sure, is proclaimed the "smartest guy alive" and required to solve the country's food crisis within a week. Joe discovers that the cornfields are irrigated and contaminated with the sports drink Brawndo. When he reintroduces the practice of watering crops, the share price of the powerful Brawndo Corporation falls and millions of people lose their jobs. Riots ensue. Joe is sentenced to death and brought to a stadium to be executed in front of the US president, a former wrestler and porn star. Rita, meanwhile,

has discovered some new shoots in the parched fields, the footage of which is broadcast to the stadium. Joe is pardoned and celebrated as a hero. Shortly afterwards he finds out that the "time machine" promised him is just a ride in an amusement park, and he can no longer return to his own present. Joe becomes president and marries his contemporary Rita, and they all live happily ever after...

*Two trajectories*—How did a moronic future become possible? The explanation is given in inserted interviews. For generations the educated elite have had no offspring, while the uneducated masses have proliferated. But in this saga of stupidity, which plays around with classicism, IQ pop, and eugenics, it never becomes clear why anything functions at all, why there's a parliament, why there's a surveillance state that tattoos its citizens with barcodes—the usual film clichés of totalitarianism, which in fact can only function by means of a ruling class that thinks and acts strategically. But dysfunctionality in IDIOCRACY appears to be ubiquitous and its politics incoherent; the country is suffocating in garbage, and hunger reigns. So not everyone is stupidly happy, because hunger makes you smart and stirs rebellion. Though the biologistic premise of the film wouldn't allow this, as IQ is inherited, and the biologically stupid would accept their status quo like animals in a zoo. But despite all citizens being integral to a gigantic techno-economic machinery, they appear to act individually. The film is pervaded by this permanent contradiction between anarchic dysfunction and "ordoliberal" totalitarianism. We can extract two ideal-type scenarios from it:

1) People are run down and live in a (post-)capitalist end state, as all areas of society—including the state apparatus—are subject to commodity fetishism, with medical services being advertised and offered in malls, for example. All social structure is a facade; wishes only exist in the form of memes, thoughts in the form of apps. The "aestheticizing of politics" (Walter Benjamin) has given way to a post-fascist aestheticizing of the aesthetic. Everything the nightmare capitalist scenario once prefigured for its opponents has come about, but it is also historically unrecognizable and politically nonsensical. The revolutionary subject

is forgotten, unthinkable, or impossible. Chance, too, is no longer in the picture. Everything conforms to redundant procedures. Psychosocial entropy holds sway. Emotion is abbreviated to sentiment, and symbols lack consistency. Flags are waved proudly, but nobody knows what they mean, only that you have to be proud of them. And even if symbols were understandable, they couldn't be squared with one's own thought and action. For example, candles on a cake would symbolize "birthday," but they wouldn't make you think of "age" and "congratulation." This scenario accords with what Musil writes about idiots: "an idiot of a certain degree is not up to forming the concept 'parents,' even though he has no trouble with the idea of 'father and mother.'" It is like communicating with Wittgenstein's lion: a lion that could speak our language wouldn't be able to communicate with us because of its lack of a shared experience on which the language is based. Countless bits of meaning don't add up to a meaningful whole. The world is fragmented into disconnected singular beings; there is no society, no culture, no history, no experience of a higher cause, and God is nothing but a gadget.

2) At the same time the film depicts a functioning power apparatus, a machinery of state control that evades its own spectacle and is dominated by an obviously not so stupid elite. This scenario shows a totalitarian pattern of strategic control over useful idiots. While in the first scenario the population is "sedated" individually and incorporated in the world of commodities, in the second scenario the hungering masses make political sense. They arise from the system's inner contradictions, and they rebel against it. But this revolutionary drive only surfaces briefly—progressively as a food riot, regressively as a lynch mob. Joe aka Not Sure, condemned as a scapegoat by the rulers, ultimately becomes the messianic hero of the future. His act of heroism consists in a "real socialist" measure: state intervention into irrigation mitigates the anger of the hungry. But the hegemonic structures remain intact. The mass movement serves merely as a menacing scenario that prepares the idiot hero for his happy end. Joe's "genius genes" will see to his offspring, the future elite. The people are happy with full bellies and empty promises. It's just another idiot in power.

*Hysterical but true*—The film suggests a ruling class and at the same time its impossibility. It isn't anarchy that rules here, but rather a *zeroed society*, symbolized in the film by the blockbuster Ass, which shows an interminable closeup of a backside (reminiscent of Yoko Ono's Fluxus film No. 4, from 1966). Unlike totalitarianism, idiocracy has no political motives. Social meaning is fragmented or incommensurate with experience, pointing to "a situation in which we can say that if individual experience is authentic, then it cannot be true; and that if a scientific or cognitive model of the same content is true, then it escapes individual experience" (Fredric Jameson). In the 1990s the director Mike Judge became famous as the creator of the MTV cartoon series BEAVIS & BUTTHEAD, which embodies a vision of an infantilized US society. With IDIOCRACY, however, he created something that comes too close for catharsis, and is too universal to seem just American. It's an idiocratic vision not because of its questionable premises but because of its capitalist realism. It frames elites and masses, rulers and the ruled, as "atypical." Idiocracy occurs neither as the Fordist dystopia of *Brave New World* (1932) nor as a comedy version of Orwell's *Nineteen Eighty-Four* (1949), but rather as a hysterical realism that reproduces its signifiers on the level of the crudest pattern. So in an idiocracy even the most outlandish metaphors replicate themselves or morph into political reality as the new normal. No surprise, then—filmic cut—that one of Donald Trump's staff members had been a professional wrestler, and his former advisor Omarosa was a TV celebrity he knew from THE APPRENTICE. And his sometime communications director Anthony Scaramucci was an almost literal realization of the Comedia dell'arte Scaramouche (*Scaramuzzo* means "skirmish" in Italian, and in English the term refers to a loudmouth or a braggart—Scaramucci was fired after an interview full of boasts and obscenities). Trump's alleged orgies or affairs with a porn star round off the picture sketched by the film ten years previously. Mike Judge's screenwriter pointed out that IDIOCRACY was the first movie that began as a feature and ended as a documentary.

*Dumbing up*—Idiocracy doesn't mean the intellectual decline that is the general assumption in mainstream critiques of capitalism. Critics of populist degeneration like to make jokes about the "power of stupidity," the "dictatorship of the stupid," or a "global dumbing down." The common narrative seems to be that we're going increasingly gaga, wearing ourselves out with market superficialities or moronic online behavior. As Sartre once noticed, this supposed revelation of bourgeois stupidity is accompanied by an attitude of superiority that creates a gap between the "moronic masses," who have been enslaved by capital, and the clever critics, who have evaded capture. If we take idiocracy merely for the rule of the "in-intelligent" (Rosset), we end up in indifferent criticism or lukewarm affirmation—along the lines of *capitalism and its antisocial technologies make us stupid, and if we only abandoned our lesser and greater stupidities, the capitalist future would be golden*. However, the "Grand Stupidity thesis" (Mitroff & Bennis) is too convenient; it distracts from the problem. It's necessary instead to remember that stupidity is the rational streak of power and idiocy the anarchic. In other words, that stupidity throws you under the rule of the big other, that is, an assumed generality of power relations that makes you do what you're "supposed" to in order to remain an integral part of what everybody thinks is right; while the idiot doesn't think, and dances around power relations or falls randomly into one position or another, whether tyrant or revolutionary, or both at once. So when talking about mental dispositions in their relation to power, we are dealing with intrinsic constellations that can't be denounced from the vantage point of an unquestioned and unmoved rationality. Rather, we should keep reason in suspense and live with an eerie suspicion that what we assume as rational may turn out to be irrational or vice versa. The task of social critique that arises here was already discussed by Adorno and Marcuse in the 1960s: it consists in capturing the inflationary irrationality (or dysrationality) and releasing it as an inner form of rationality; it consists in including the critic in the object of criticism, and at the same time recognizing the object of criticism as constitutive of the rationality of knowledge. This task is somewhat comparable to the academic understanding of humor: a theory of humor that doesn't make you laugh is ineffective, and a theory of humor that does make you laugh isn't serious. So the skill is to find wit when engaging the subject—somewhere between Henri Bergson and Monty Python.

*Default society*—The above cinematic metaphor is realized in the imagination of a future society in which, on the Judgment Day of political economy, we have all become the useful idiots of win-win market reflexes embedded in a long-term lose-lose reality. Only in this sense is it reasonable to discuss idiocy as a political paradigm, namely as a relation in which the criteria of power become muddled or paradoxical. As Félix Guattari put it in 1982 in conversation with Sylvère Lotringer: "We are currently in a phase of considerable turmoil, a phase one could call pre-revolutionary, although I'd rather define it as a 'molecular' revolution, where virtually no one can control anything anymore." In this sense an idiocracy is the self-sabotage of power as power. It can take the form of a capitalist post-capitalism or a "postcapitalist interregnum" (Wolfgang Streeck). Ethical emptiness, inflation of values, communication blockades, discursive confusion, political vanities, self-cancellation, cancellation of others, cognitive overload, and so on are the system's default mode. But what system? The one capitalism means many things in the meantime, some of them non-capitalist or anti-capitalist—because capitalism itself is the giver of meaning through which late-modern agendas are articulated, whether as *disaster capitalism, finance capitalism, cognitive capitalism, semio-capitalism, cultural capitalism, surveillance capitalism, crisis capitalism, narco-capitalism, late capitalism, cyber-capitalism, post-capitalism, chaos capitalism* … "Money makes time," reads Don DeLillo's *Cosmopolis* (2003), but capital creates signifiers. When Jean-Luc Nancy, in *The Sense of the World* (1993), writes that "there is no longer any assignable signification of 'world,'" that "the 'world' is subtracting itself, bit by bit, from the entire regime of signification available to us," this doesn't apply to the inexhaustible capitalist arsenal of signs and "isms" that continually rearticulate the zeroed society, the "zero" of which isn't simply a matter of an "original position," as posited by John Rawls—that is, an imaginary starting point of the social contract—but a permanently anticipated endpoint, if you will, an uplifting demise or a melancholy happy end.

# POLITICAL IDIOCY

*ἰδιο-λόγος: a particular way of speaking and
investigating; an official rank in ancient Egypt.*

*No longer*—The idiocratic condition seems to be paradigmatic for a development stage of the late-modern subject, which wears itself out between total particularization and total generalization. It's no longer a
question of the grand narratives of the Enlightenment, but of finding
historical, aesthetic, or logical contours within an unnamable whole.
How can individuals seeking meaning hold their own against the wave
of meaninglessness? The grand narratives don't disappear without
trace; they deplete into the discourse of specialists—economists, epi-
demiologists, or climatologists as authorities in saving the world, for
example—or reproduce themselves blindly at the pulse of the market like everything else. This affects our communicative behavior:
the majority speaks in the manner of the minority, if its dominance is
threatened, and a minority speaks in the manner of the majority when
it wishes for dominance. Whatever the difficulty of balancing out the
global and the local in our lives, it is also increasingly difficult to com-
bine individual with general knowledge. Political idiocy in this context
is no misguided calculation or blunder but rather a strange form of success, namely the unifying of the general and the particular *without relating them to a world*. Or conversely it asserts a world without relating
the general to the particular. Either we generalize to the point of plati-
tude or we lose ourselves in discourse (or both), but we lay claim to the
entire scope of meaning. The incongruence of abstract knowledge and
industrial production that Karl Marx outlined in his *Grundrisse* (1858),
and that echoes today in debates around the New or Green Economy,

is reflected here: the generalization of labor through the collapse of the exchange value can no longer be reconciled with the specifics of post-industrial production. In the advancement of abstract knowledge to a productive force, the Italian philosopher Paolo Virno sees an epochal self-sabotage of the law of value. There is an idiocratic state of affairs here, in as much as "the full factual realization of the tendency described by Marx"—that is, "production based on exchange value breaks down"—has no liberating consequences. According to Virno, the late-modern incongruency of knowledge and labor "has given rise to new and stable forms of power" instead of leading to "communism," in the Marxian sense of a stateless society of free individuals. Zygmunt Bauman's idea of "liquid modernity" points to a similar self-sabotage of the zeitgeist, namely a modernity that "liquifies" the very foundations on which it was premised. The incongruity of the general and the particular is nothing new, but it continually "feels" new because the acceleration of work processes and the simultaneous lengthening of production times are increasingly shortening the product cycles of knowledge creation. This doesn't lead to the "affectivity of the here and now," as the German sociologist Andreas Reckwitz would put it, but more to the *affectivity of the soon* or the *affectivity of the no-longer,* as I would put it. Not only is every last-but-one product out of date but also every last-but-one sentence. What do I send on ahead to the next-but-one sentence? What does it mean to infer from past premises?

*Short circuit*—The incongruence of the general and the particular, which reproduces itself and ensures a generalization of the particular, translates politically as confusion: talking points are subject to a cycle of meaning, and in the competition of public opinion the point at which a sentence intervenes in the cycle to make sense is arbitrary. And so in an idiocracy a commitment to free speech is the surest way to silence others. In the US, for example, the free-speech debate has become a means of agitation to create a platform for conspiracy narratives or hate speech that excludes the dissent of others. The "politically incorrect" permit no politically incorrect criticism of incorrectness. Their self-sabotage lies in the use of a liberal media landscape to question humanist standards, so as to put one over on the liberal mainstream, failing to recognize that the same humanist standards also apply to those who wish to abolish them. Their questioning puts them at a disadvantage, but at the same time, and feeling it to be the absolute opposite, they want to live it out as "world ethos." This is a reason why they dwell in global conspiracies—they need a *secret* world in order to compensate for the lack of a *sacred* one. A fragment of thought—a "standpoint," an "identity"—is projected onto the whole here, without sensing the incongruity that equally affects every protagonist in the global structure of knowledge, power, and labor. The consequence isn't solidarity among the confused, but a crazy dance of diversity that disguises itself in everyday politics as "conflicting opinions." The "conflict," however, is based more on the incongruity of the general and the particular than on substance. We believe that we believe something, or we are convinced that we are convinced of something, so these metabeliefs and hearsay convictions clash on undefined grounds—in this context the conspiracy cult QAnon is quite literally an admission of nothingness. Alternatively, people are led to call for an action that contradicts their belief in the name of their belief, like self-declared "patriots" storming the Capitol, Black Lives Matter riots causing Black deaths, or pro-life activists assaulting planned parenthood facilities and wreaking carnage in the name of unborn life. The practice of self-sabotage can't easily be ascribed to a general shortcoming or mere performative contradiction, because the power of the particular it depicts is continually reproduced or turned on itself. Idiocracy shouldn't therefore be reduced to the failures of the American experiment or to political figures trolling the system. I focus on the United States because this country has proved to be a reliable messenger of what is to come in terms of global development, not least due to the success of its cultural imperialism, the "Fourth Rome" and the *pax americana,* its historically unrivaled military presence. By singling it out, essentially, we include everything else. Those who shout "Death to America" do so on US terms with US technology. Analogously, the best-defined "non-Western" art is exhibited globally in galleries shaped by the Western white-cube paradigm. Yet this world of worlds is more than the US or the West as colonial signifiers can encompass. It points to a condition that short-circuits the empire with itself and plays out in a commodified global online arena that is more than the sum of its symbols. With the help of Web almighty, we might therefore claim that everything anywhere in this world of worlds flows into the next best meme and a platform-bargaining in which radicality and mainstream become aspects of a single tribunal of taste—just like the trial in IDIOCRACY.

*Confusionism*—Just as the idiot isn't an invective idiot but a real one, so is idiocratic confusion not "psychological" but real. In November 2018 liberals throughout the US took to the streets to signal their support for the conservative attorney general Jeff Sessions because they saw his dismissal as political influence of the judiciary by the Trump administration. One protestor carried a placard saying she couldn't believe she was having to demonstrate for Sessions. Meaning that she was demonstrating for the reinstatement of a politician in particular whose reinstatement she generally opposed. This was completely rational and at the same time idiotic, because today a political position can often only be expressed in self-sabotaging terms, no matter how strategically justified it is. This was epitomized during the Brexit debates in the British Parliament in 2019, when the prime minister wanted to avoid a new election but aimed for one procedurally, while the leader of the opposition had been calling for a new election for years but refused to table his demands. I'm not saying this is irrational or unjustified versus rational and justified, as if there existed a rational choice. I'm saying that in an idiocracy fragmented intelligence becomes the political norm, and the political norm the pathology of a normality that does away with strategic tit for tat. Here we only have irrational choices that are all "true," no matter what. This tautology was perfectly realized on May 21, 2016, when Russian hackers from a troll farm in Saint Petersburg organized an anti-Islam demonstration in front of the Da'wah Center in Houston, to stop the "Islamization of Texas," and the same hackers on the same day called for a counterdemo, which attracted thousands of US citizens and led to clashes between the two groups. According to the Senate Intelligence Committee Chairman Richard Burr the proxy war cost Russia about $200. Again, the point here is not to ridicule the supposed stupidity or naivity of the surrogate protesters but to see their confusion as an *objectively idiotic* one, exemplary for global politics as such. From this idiocratic angle we can understand the bulk of "populist" figures like Silvio Berlusconi, Donald Trump, Jair Bolsonaro, Boris Johnson, Recip Erdogan, Narendra Modi, Rodrigo Duterte, Vladimir Putin, and other adepts in merging strategy and idiocy. These tautological figures perfectly symbolize the failure of the general and the particular to find a common ground. Whether "America first" demagogy, Hindu nationalism, or the Russian "Eurasian" empire—to put it in terms of the "Putin whisperer" Aleskandr Dugin—all identitarian movements are driven by idiocratic ineffect: they make way by not making sense. Russia's twenty-first-century autocracy neatly embeds nineteenth-century bourgeois cultural identity, the Soviet empire, the Romanov monarchy, the Orthodox church, and an internationally operating oligarchy, all under the umbrella of the Russian nation. And doesn't Trump's version of "America First" include too a contradictory mix of neocons and economic nationalists, anti-Semites and Zionists, evangelicals and never-churchers? This amalgamation, however, also points to a productive aspect of political idiocy: a creativity that drives the political logos towards previously unknown—or shall we say "unpresidented"—horizons.

*Political thermodynamics*—Idiocracy shows up the abstract but real political and economic consequences of a world that is no longer worldlike. As Félix Guattari observed in the 1980s, capital, as the "integral of power formations," has become a global semiotic operator, continually bringing forth pseudo-worlds and pseudo-collectives based on what Marx called "the perfected form of the general equivalent," aka money. Many thinkers in the Marxist tradition have been bothered by capitalist totality, but Guattari and others emphasize the semiotic aspects of subjectivation. The function of the semiotic operator consists in maintaining "cool" systems of technological and financial dominance. From these evolve "warm" humanlike complexes characterized, according to Paolo Virno, by "the immediate connection between production and ethicality, 'structure' and 'superstructure,' the revolutionizing of the work process and sentiments, technologies and the emotional tonalities, material development, and culture." Here we can paraphrase Ernst Bloch's metaphor of the "heat flow" and speak of the *thermal flow* of capitalism: patterns of alienation are covered over by humanizing symbols and ideologemes. This can already be seen in popular language: "How's the company *doing*?" "How will markets *react*?" "The economy is *suffering*," "Will the markets *recover*?" "The markets don't *like* it!" Conversely, phrases referring to people are financialized: How much do I *invest* in a relationship? How much can I *get out* of a meeting? A French saying urges you not only to enjoy your holidays but to *profit* by them (*Profite bien de tes vacances*). The anthropomorphization of capital is determined by a reciprocal valorization of life and rationalization of emotions. As Eva Illouz puts it: "It is this progressive fusion of the market repertoires and languages of the self during the twentieth century which I have called 'emotional capitalism.' In the culture of emotional capitalism, emotions have become entities to be evaluated, inspected, discussed, bargained, quantified, and commodified." Warm feeling meets cool calculation. In the 1990s publications such as George Ritzer's *McDonaldization of Society* (1993) were still looking at the culture of operationalization and optimization that was the basis of capitalist emotionality. But the patterns go further back. Historically the effects of Guattari's global semiotic operator are associated with the simultaneity of a territorialization aka "particularization" and a deterritorialization aka "generalization" of capital: on the one hand the uprooting of the local "modes of semiotization of powers" involved in the generalization of signs, which create coldness, and on the other the rooting of general significators in national frameworks, which create a specific temperature: patriotism is warm, globalization is cold. It could be called a "political thermodynamics." Politicians also have their temperatures: Joe Biden ≈ warm, Donald Trump ≈ warm, Angela Merkel ≈ cold. Jair Bolsonaro ≈ warm, Vladimir Putin ≈ cold. Rodrigo Duterte ≈ warm, Victor Orban ≈ cold, and so on. The thermal metaphors don't come from nowhere: they were used by neoclassical economists in the late nineteenth century to objectivize political economy into a science, as Philip Mirowski has shown in his book *More Heat than Light* (1989). Hence also the metaphors of economic "equilibrium" or market "over-heating." Just as the "new capitalism" leads to anthropomorphization and/or emotionalization, the global level is dominated by a thermody-namic cycle that links the heat generators with their cold source. It is then "no coincidence that most of the newspapers promoting the na-tivist agenda, whipping up hatred against immigrants and thundering about sovereignty, are owned by billionaire tax exiles, living offshore" (George Monbiot). The one exile rails against the other, tax versus bor-der. The universal aspirations of present-day nationalisms are similarly characterized by generalization and localization, undercooling and overheating—Michael Billig distinguishes here between "hot" and "cold" nationalism in his work *Banal Nationalism* (1995). The nation state is territorial and sometimes "hotly contested," but the territorial signature is planetary; that is, "cold" dominates. The *space-of-places* and the *space-of-flows* (Hendrikse & Fernandez), that is, the national and the transnational, oscillate to form a thermodynamic pattern. So all national anthems sound the same, for example, because they have to be recognizable as such internationally. Many South American anthems sound like Italian operas because that was what they were modeled on, or they were written by Italian composers. The national anthems of Turkey and Israel have the same basic melody. Arabic an-thems are based on Western march music because national anthems are a Western invention. Anyone wanting to raise the temperature by distancing him or herself from the West could whistle or dance instead of standing up straight. But nobody does. Even hostile cultures seem to agree on the question of patriotic decorum. The anthems instill a warm feeling, although, as Zarathustra says, "State is the name of the coldest of all cold monsters."

*Exterior meaning*—Political idiocy means that territoriality and planetary generalization don't establish congruent structures, that is, that the thermal cycle is dysfunctional—the result of a political "climate change." This ultimately comes down to what Jean-Luc Nancy wrote in *The Sense of the World* (1998) in reply to the "end of history" after the collapse of the Eastern bloc: "There is no longer any world: no longer a *mundus*, a *cosmos*, a composed and complete order (from) within which one might find a place, a dwelling, and the elements of an orientation. [...] In other words, there is no longer any sense of the world." Today we must pluralize this diagnosis: there are no *senses* of the world because of a kind of globally prevailing locked-in syndrome that makes it increasingly difficult to reconcile the interior movement of capital with its exterior effects. In this constellation global activists and backyard conservatives, for example, are no longer opposites, as every protagonist needs an exterior in relation to a postulated interior and vice versa. And so, as Zygmunt Bauman points out in his analysis of late modernity, belief in an achievable telos of history, a social order in which everything and everyone has found its place, has dissipated. It is therefore necessary to understand the aimless movement and lack of sense(s), as Fredric Jameson, for example, suggested with his "cognitive mapping." Today it is a matter of navigating the idiocratic territory and getting to the bottom of its (de)territorializing effects. To use a technological analogy: geotagging technologies define the unique standpoint of the subject, but the information gained doesn't lead to a better location of the subject in the world; it reproduces apparent presence and spatio-temporal undepictability instead. Even the complete acquisition of all the world's coordinates wouldn't describe a world, only something like one. The increasingly frequent GPS pranks by military and private aircraft, leaving phallic drawings on the radar by means of their flightpaths, and similar stunts by hobbyists, are microscopic indications of interaction of big data with the uncoordinated world. They can also be understood as the warmth-creating self-sabotage of the coordinating system, although the subversive form has no subversive content.

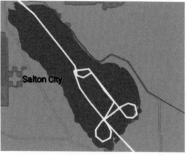

Reality mining—GPS-tracking of cellphone users in San Francisco (Sense Networks, 2008) and flightpath of a US jet fighter over California, 2018.

What the IT sector has called *reality mining* (the use of big data to map and predict human behavior) thus becomes semiotic feedback on an individual level. Some years ago, for example, a female American jogger began posting her daily routes in the form of penises on her webpage— the phallus, apart from indicating the daily symbolic presence of patriarchy, here also being the symbol that comes most naturally to infantile rationale, similarly to the middle finger. Other joggers followed her example with more complex renderings, and so the new discipline of GPS art was born. The unpolitical nonsense is political on another level, however, and the arbitrary phenomenon central. It's the creative attempt to give exterior meaning to one's aimless wanderings: rather vulgar than non-existent. And so everyone continually produces something rather than nothing, only to be somewhere sometime. This has a political counterpart in David Goodhart's *The Road to Somewhere* (2017). Goodhart deals with the political antinomies brought about in late modernity with the resulting antagonism between "somewheres" and "anywheres," that is, between the located and the unlocated people, only that we have to realize now that the located are lost and the anywheres are nowhere. The biggest of all big data won't ensure a safe landing in this world. Quite the opposite: the above depictive concept was originated by American artist Dennis Oppenheim, who had jet fighters draw spirals in the sky in the 1970s—a flight pattern typical of crashing planes.

*Anything goes, this time for real*—Instead of committed solidarity, the molecularization of power increasingly brings forth politics aimed at individual self-legitimation. This tendency is conducive to the idiocratic form, that is, as a "shift from social pluralism to the dogmatic application of privatised solutions" (Neil Curtis). In drawing at random from the global reservoir, idiotized individuals can adopt the most arbitrary positions. They may see themselves as one among many, but they don't accept any haphazardness of world events that would compel their solidarity with others. Instead they stylize themselves as protagonists with unique selling points—Nero's last words were "What an artist dies in me!" Self-pity from which arises a sense of entitlement and a right to be right no matter what, as if the scholastic formula for ontic truth, *adaequatio rei ad intellectum*, which requires a "match of thing to intellect" (or vice versa for logical truth), could do without matching. In other words, things have to adapt to the idiot because he creates them in the same way that he himself is created. This is why self-politics can be volatile and inherently contradictory, can collapse its discourses and proclaim the collapse *as* discourse. Anything goes—but this time it's meant seriously: "We turn to the most general categories in order to equip ourselves for the most varied specific situations, no longer having at our disposal any 'special' or sectorial ethical-communicative codes" (Virno).

*The ghost of the state*—The incongruence of the particular and the general is also one of the reasons why neoliberalism, as a discourse of denationalization, was a chimaera from the very beginning. The deregulation of the markets, the blurring of the boundaries between work and life, the social distortions of globalization, the financialization of all areas of society, the atomization of the social, the commercialization of the cultural, and so on, reproduced the blind fusion of capital and happiness. This was a large-scale self-sabotage, for a state abolishing itself is the ultimate state. Nothing shouts "more government!" more than government deliberately reducing its economic influence (this also applies to Marx's supposedly apolitical administrators of the "withered-away" state). It isn't the absence of state controls that is neoliberal, but the private-sector maneuvering to protect the state—also true of Robert Nozick's libertarian version of the minarchist minimal state. As long as there is a guaranteeing legal system, and as long as there are nation-states with their military securing territorial sovereignty and so on, there is always no more and no less than 100% state—it's a similarly popular myth that humans only access a fragment of their cerebral capacity, which, if we follow the above logic, would justify calls for "more brain!" or "less brain!" As Fernand Braudel once put it: "Capitalism triumphs when it becomes identified with the state, when it becomes part of the state." Even Friedrich von Hayek recognized this, when he weighed up capitalism and Stalinism and saw that both systems, each in its way, sought an étatist paradise on earth. The insight was that international deterritorialized "offshore finance is woven from the sovereign fabric of states, anchoring the capitalist world of property (*dominium*) through the rampant commercialization of state sovereignty (*imperium*)" (Hendrikse & Fernandez). Zygmunt Bauman writes of a "statism without a state." The self-abolishing, self-abstracting but still insisting state—the "ghost" of statism—is both the guarantee of universal reason and the patron of a libidinous immersion in risk capitalism—whether offshore or onshore, online or offline—which in turn finishes off universal reason. We live in neoliberalism, but neoliberalism doesn't exist. Where do we live?

*Higher blindness*—As a radical consequence of late-capitalist subjectivation, idiocracy stands in a "society of singularities" (Reckwitz). So it's also possible to speak of an "idiot paradigm" (Matthew Poole) to paraphrase a "paradigm of paradigmlessness" in which the main social distinctions lose their meaning and all social mobility is sabotaged, as it is simultaneously delegated to the singular individual and the totality of "one," that is, one is completely differentiated oneself, so differentiated discourse can be dispensed with. In the words of Matthew Poole, the contradictions of the idiot paradigm go hand in hand with the contradictions of political economy: "Capitalist economic relations appear to be so blindingly complex and intertwined with all aspects of life that we appear not to be able to discern cause-and-effect relationships between social, political, ethical, or economic activities in the world." The diagnosis can be tied in with those of Thomas Piketty and others, who ascribe the increasing discrepancy of income to an exponential growth in blindness that is "overpowering" real growth. This is spurred by a "meritocratic extremism" that brings forth supermanagers with exorbitant earnings. Referring to Marx, Moishe Postone emphasized that the capital form of society had a "blind character," and that capital represented the perpetual self-reproduction of value as an abstraction that relentlessly produced scapegoats, be they Jews, Muslim refugees, Eastern European migrants, or other minorities, in order to match capitalist desire with global knowledge. The scapegoats are the meritocratic counterpart of the supermanagers: both groups, migrants and managers, "do nothing" for society, but are negatively (or positively) sanctioned in order to distract from the causes of income discrepancy. But capital needs both groups so as to maintain the dynamic of meritocratic values. Refugee centers and financial centers are two aspects of one and the same structure, two aspects of a global movement out of and into capital.

*Disintegration*—Political idiocy denotes a conflict between the particular and the general, the incongruence of abstract knowledge and experience, the short-circuiting of radicality and mainstream in a world of worlds. It refers to a general confusion based on particular truths, on the humanizing "monstrosity" of capital and adjustments to its "thermodynamics," on the creation of pseudo-signifiers that emulate a non-existing place in the world. The idiocratic *We* is nowhere to be found, neither are its *Is*. As with the above polarization of managers and migrants, superfluous and moneyed subjects float lifelessly in the sea of the more-or-less, which at times they themselves produce, comparable with the self-realizing value of capital as an "automatic subject" (Marx). According to Bernard Stiegler, this development shows signs of a disintegration that typifies existence in the twenty-first century.

It could be called a *post-existential condition*. It consists in the subjugation of the individual to the imperatives of the global economy. This not only leads to a permanent moral and spiritual crisis, as Stiegler emphasizes, but also corresponds to the above-discussed self-sabotage of the law of value through automatization and abstract labor. It's therefore no surprise that AI technology has become the main signifier of human affairs in recent years, and that in 2022 a Google employee "fell in love" with a consumer algorithm, believing it had gained consciousness. For Stiegler every person is characterized by an "intimate and secret" relationship to him or herself, which he describes with Freud as "primary narcissism." This is the reason why every subjugation to the global order leads to dissatisfaction and a loss of confidence in the future. So we need to delegate the future to human-like projects intended to emulate what we have lost. The loss of confidence also reinforces swarm behavior instead of restoring the intimate relationship. This is why idiotism and conformism aren't opposites. For today's swarm the world exists as an exaggeration which requires decisions that are impossible for individuals to make. Its creed sacrifices truth to acquire new knowledge, be it no knowledge and no life, at all—*cogito quia absurdum, ergo non sum.*

# THE WILL TO ABSURDITY

*2 × 2 = green*
Heinz von Foerster

*Everyone everything everywhere*—The curiosity cabinet of online idiocy shows the meme of a man rinsing his car with a hosepipe in the pouring rain. In contrast to a gardener standing in the rain, annoyed that he can't try out his new sprinkler, the car-washer is stoic: he isn't going to let the weather tell him when he can wash his car. So he goes on rinsing with his own weather. Until his deed—I pull the image out of its frame—becomes an autotelic formula, purposing nothing but itself. Would the man wash his car in a flood, or if the world were about to end? Perhaps at that very moment, for in the face of the end of the world all deeds become equal and nothing is ridiculous any more. The man could plant an apple tree like Martin Luther or dash off a tweet. Everything that happened would be conceived in terms of the end of the world and be absolutely normal; that is, any act would be as incidental as it was radical. Don't all political projects now have the eschatological defiance of our car-washer? Isn't it so that an undefined end time is projecting into our present, in which every act creates its own significance, no matter how insignificant it is? The defiant car-washer is the symbol of a coming time. A time in which metaphors become real, in which the real is absurd and the absurd real. A time in which the wisdom of Voltaire's Pangloss cuts capers: "These individual misfortunes are for the general good: the more individual misfortunes there are, the more everything is as it ought to be." Today's world is turning in Voltaire's grave. Here's what *Forbes* magazine had to say in November 2018: "Surging Wealth Inequality Is A Happy Sign That Life Is Becoming Much More Convenient." The stream of absurdity from all sources is due to a new type of idiot, an epochal meme fulfilling the prophesy of the one-eyed sage that everyone will know everything when every individual no longer knows anything.

*Real & absurd*—"'No man but an idiot would pick up that little hammer if he could use a big hammer.' [...] 'Well [...], no man but an idiot did,'" reads a short story by G.K. Chesterton. Until someone has hammered out the absurd, it doesn't occur to anyone that it could also be real. But what is absurdity? If you like to think in terms of conceptual fashions, you might link it with a particular period of time. Then it appears that life was only absurd in the 1930s, 40s, 50s, and 60s, but not later, when the word never crossed anyone's lips (intellectual dependency on the lips of others seems absurd by itself). But isn't what Eugène Ionesco wrote still true? "Cut off from his religious, metaphysical, and transcendental roots, man is lost; all his actions become senseless, absurd, useless." Have the roots grown back? No. Jihadists and pre-emptive defenders of the West in particular attest to modern forsakenness in their exaggerated pathos, in overshooting God and nation to land on an uninhabitable planet. And the "theatre of the absurd"? Isn't all theater absurd? Don't its participants suspect that stage life is senseless, and isn't this why they are in defiance of a time becoming increasingly hostile to art? Our extent of action is the indication of a final perspective (why? what for?) that we can't oppose with transcendence. And so we oppose it with our immanence. Absurdity, according to the American philosopher Thomas Nagel, consists in "the collision between the seriousness with which we take our lives, and our capacity to step back, look at things from a wider perspective, and see how ridiculously contingent the activities that fill our lives really are." We open our hands and realize there's nothing there, that the seriousness of life can be continually done away with.

*Unidirectionality*—The philosopher and physicist Ernst Mach once described the universe as something that can't be reflected—it has no outside—and that only exists in this one-sidedness. Therefore the question of the meaning of life is posed in the singular. No one asks about the *meanings* of life, because these are life itself. According to Mach's compatriot, the Austrian philosopher Otto Weininger, the "unidirectionality of time also contains the reason why our need for immortality only extends to the future (not back to life before we were born). Because of it, we have little interest in our state before birth, but a great deal in our state after death." Meaning has one direction, which is why it is the one meaning of life. It's difficult to imagine religious extremists who blow themselves up in order to reach a state before their birth. Human life breaks new ground in this unidirectionality of time, like waves breaking on a rocky shore. In his catalogue of paradoxes, Kierkegaard writes that truth is recognizable by absurdity; that is, a paradox that voids reflection and is only sublated in faith. At the bottom of life, as far as human beings seek truth, there is an "absolute absurdity" (Sartre) that can nowhere be revoked—and yet, in a life's struggle, is permanently revoked—which confronts the meaning of life with its meaninglessness.

*The new idiot*—At this point Deleuze and Guattari see a shifting of the second realm in front of the first: "The old idiot wanted indubitable truths at which he could arrive by himself: in the meantime he would doubt everything, even that 3 + 2 = 5; he would doubt every truth of Nature. The new idiot has no wish for indubitable truths; he will never be 'resigned' to the fact that 3 + 2 = 5 and wills the absurd [...]. The old idiot wanted truth, but the new idiot wants to turn the absurd into the highest power of thought—in other words, to create." The idiot of the first order, the old idiot, sees the truth in his initial view of the world. The new idiot, regardlessly, not only turns all circumstances into "his thing" but in doing so makes a mockery of doing. That's creative, as it includes the preconditions of creation in the deed itself. At the same time he reveals in himself "the overwhelming and ineradicable, unquenchable thirst for creative destruction" (Bauman). So it's not by chance that the new idiot defines the modern figurations of absurdity, as did Père Ubu in the cultural production of the fin de siècle, Dada until 1922, the surrealists in the interwar years, or the situationists after 1945. The atomization of styles and movements retains their inherent idiot types as something like a cultural residue of the present. To put it differently, the new idiot takes on the role of the conceptual person with whom we now cope with the life's absurdity, and with whom we adjudge the meaningfulness (or lessness) of the world. In the cultural sector, where the new idiot is dialectically pervaded by types of the first order, that is, where absurdity is conceived from or as the beginning, it can be observed as a form of "time activism," becoming the idiot hero of its specific time. Where it is projected apocalyptically onto the end, it appears as the symptom of a dysfunctional epoch of events, of idiocracy, which shields itself from the same absurdity that it constantly produces: the counterproductivity you need in order to be productive, or vice versa, "conditioning through absurdity," as Frantz Fanon once called it. The absurd has gone out of fashion today; it is no longer "understood" because we now live this side of absurdity and under the spell of the new idiot, who constantly undermines or shapes the procedures of power.

*Trickle-down ontology*—In this light the above-described car-washer is also the realized metaphor of a system whose truth dribbles down more relentlessly than rain—of a system in which every deed has the character of a moral-boosting economic slogan to keep the planetary rain machine going. No matter what the message of the rain propaganda is, in the product scheme of metaphysical "automobilism," he is actor and aut(h)o(r) in his defiant rinsing, an indeterminate subject who will ensure that his own water will see off the alien water along with all other competition. And if we can imagine the sun illuminating the scene, the car's gleaming paint will be a symbol of perfection, the material equivalent of the reality of the absurd. The new idiot is as happy in his activity as a freshly bathed child in a towel. All things and beings inhabit a natural cycle. They evaporate, trickle down, become rivers and flow into the stream of happiness whose intensity depends on the increasing unhappiness of all individuals. There are so many therapists, consultants, coaches, and advisers today because of the need to heave these unhappy folk onto the level of universal happiness. If they succeeded, universal unhappiness would be perfect.

*Realization*—The will to absurdity doesn't merely refer to the transformation of the conceptual person of the idiot; it also emulates the substance of political reality. It is the threshold at which the metaphor of the idiot becomes real. The "realization of the metaphor" isn't just a literary stylistic device, as in Russian formalism; it is also, as outlined by Dubravka Ugrešić in *The Culture of Lies* (1998) and Suzan Jacoby in *The Age of American Unreason in a Culture of Lies* (2018), the indication of an underlying fundamental conflict. Where metaphors become real and, as Ugrešić shows for the post-Yugoslavian conflict, imagined borders in poetry and popular culture become incentives for warfare, a "war" is already raging on the level of the literalness of the sign, on the level of the crudest pattern. Jacoby's historical analysis of American public life alludes to this in conceiving the variety of social phenomena in a single motif underlying the American divide: "America is now ill with a powerful mutant strain of intertwined ignorance, anti-rationalism, and anti-intellectualism—as opposed to the recognizable cyclical strains of the past—the virulence of the current outbreak is inseparable from an unmindfulness that is, paradoxically, both aggressive and passive." Jacoby calls it the age of unreason. But, strictly speaking, the age of the idiot is neither reasonable nor unreasonable—or it's both at the same time.

*Transcendental Trump*—One central motif of existentialism is running up against "absurd walls," as Camus describes the Sisyphean task. The new idiot is someone who calls for an ultimate unassailable wall, as Donald Trump did in a literal realization of the metaphor. Whether wall, steak, or insult, the new idiot throws his idiosyncrasies to the others, like the god in ZARDOZ (1974) throws weapons to the tribe. And now everyone wants these special things, like customers at a sale, no matter how absurd they are. And so these special things become the new raison d'être, because everyone is under the spell of the new idiot and wants to become a new idiot and finally does become a new idiot and reproduces new idiots in turn. The world is populated by countless little Trumps running around with special things. But all these little Trumps and these special things are animated by the same idiot type that arose long before Trump and will exist long after him, all driven by the same special-thing mechanism. The new idiot refutes himself in a single breath without noticing the slightest contradiction, states a position without having one, and boasts about something he has no idea of. He thinks he can control procedures over which he has no influence, speaks of truth without having a concept of it—this is why he brands it as, say, "Truth Social." He is unaware of lies because there are only affirmations, of negations because there are only opposites, of defeats because there are only victories, of baldness because there is only hair. His prime concern is to utilize impossibility and claim it as reality. His rationality consists of rations. And here too lies his epic narrative: doing for the sake of doing, but never doubting or feeling existentially. We recall the words of Bayer's *idiot a*: "what i do happens, but i shouldn't do it. it happens." The traditionally absurd deed is in vain because it gains its meaning from an effort which has to fail, just as the liberal hope of a human capitalism must be continually disappointed in order to keep itself going. Finite beings perish. The new will to absurdity, however, is infinite and impossible, and therefore on another level destructive and creative. The new idiot is a moving mover swimming in a world of flowing object relations. Although he recognizes categories, he consistently ends up in self-contradiction or finds the quickest way to put his foot in his mouth. During a 2022 fundraiser Trump said to a Gays for Trump representative, "You don't look gay," to the apparent laughter of those represented. This groundlessness is where the new idiot's aversion to "political correctness" or his love of the "uneducated" comes from. The tyranny of semiotic operators defines the new "free thinking" of the arbitrary: the provisional is taken for the absolute so as to claim a false freedom. The new idiot suspects semantic derivations. He wants something that doesn't exist: the largest in the smallest, the persistent in the short-lived, culture in globalization, globalization in culture. He has a secret with no content (*conspiracy*), is convinced by something he doesn't believe in (*patriotism*), aspires to something without having a clear idea of what it is (*identity*), and even the grand ego he prides himself on is short-circuited by his id. Or he has no ego but he's going for an id. That's his wall. Being a people, becoming president, protecting the West, killing drug-dealers, closing borders, shutting down the Internet, telling the truth, drinking bleach, storming the Capitol: it's the burning imagination of an adolescent before visiting his first brothel. These patterns of thought and behavior may be found in leaders great and small. Their clearest articulation, however, is in artistic modernism. Albert Jarry created the prototype of this modern wannabe in his pot-bellied Père Ubu, a figure who raises entitlement to the highest art form. Like Papa Trump, Papa Ubu doesn't want to be king at first, but others cajole him. But the others are also him. And when he does become king, he knows that he always wanted to. But he doesn't know what being a king means, or even if being king is a "thing." Ubu wants to enrich himself, but there's no aim in it. He is prodded, and that's what he wants, or he brags about something but then doesn't want it anymore. But there are no buts in Ubu, just a big butt like in the blockbuster in IDIOCRACY. The new idiot progresses in bewilderment to new powers and maxims. Himself acephalous, while robbing others of their brains, he asserts himself where others see the emperor's new clothes. As soon as the least resistance occurs, our imaginary commander in chief collapses. Ubu crawls sniveling into the bunker or under the table, and yells "pshit!" An enraged citizen king, a blue white collar. As a contemporary critic wrote about the premiere of *Ubu Roi* on December 9, 1896, at the Théâtre de l'Œuvre in Paris: "Despite the idiotic plot and indifferent structure, a new genre has emerged from an extraordinary and cruel childhood fantasy. Père Ubu is among us. [...] You will never be rid of him; he will haunt you, and you will encounter him again and again. He will become a popular legend of the lower instincts." The new idiot knows neither imprisonment nor calamity, and if he ends up behind bars, another one of his kind will become president. The same other.

## DIALECTIC OF INCOMPETENCE

*Give me ten men like Clouseau and I could destroy the entire world.*
Commissioner Dreyfus, A SHOT IN THE DARK (1965)

*Groundlessness*—Ortega y Gasset discerned a basic condition of the new idiot in the early twentieth century: "There appears for the first time in Europe a type of man who does not want to give reasons or to be right, but simply shows himself resolved to impose his opinions. This is the new thing: the right not to be reasonable, the 'reason of unreason,'" writes the author of *The Revolt of the Masses* (1930). This new Ubu-esque condition, in whose planetary echo chamber myriads of online commentaries now resound, is expressed in an incompetent claim to competence: "The average man finds himself with 'ideas' in his head, but he lacks the faculty of ideation. He has no conception even of the rare atmosphere in which ideas live. He wishes to have opinions, but is unwilling to accept the conditions and presuppositions that underlie all opinion." Before the onset of postmodern anxiety, Ortega y Gasset doesn't anticipate the progressive history of incompetence. He fails to notice that the above-average idiot, raising his ugly head as an "intellectual idiot" (Taleb), joins his average counterpart from the start. Nor does he see that the abstract processes of capital determine the groundlessness of both the absurd king and the absurd citizen. A dialectic of incompetence can be seen here: if, as Commissioner Dreyfus suggests in the above quotation, only ten Clouseaus were needed to destroy the entire world, they could scarcely be described as incompetent. "There is a great gift that ignorance has to bring to anything," replied Orson Welles when asked how he had managed to make CITIZEN KANE (1941) at the age of twenty-three. But here we should speak of a kind of directed ignorance, an ignorance that "knows" and "wants" something. However, if ignorance goes along with directed inability we enter the mysterious realm of idiocracy. Uri Geller is a case in point. It was his *inability* to demonstrate his paranormal abilities under controlled conditions, during his infamous appearance on the Johnny Carson Show, that led to the Geller hype of the 1970s. Viewers saw his failure as proof that he was not an illusionist but a "real psychic," as professional magicians never bungle a trick, while authentic psychics make mistakes; they are "naturally" supernatural, so to speak.

*Undercompetence*—In an idiocracy you aren't called to be merely incompetent but to be sufficiently *undercompetent*. This assertion has found its way into economic wisdom, as can be seen in numerous offbeat publications such as *Freakonomics* (2005) or *Think Like a Freak* (2014), by "rogue economists" Steven D. Levitt and Stephen J. Dubner. Here "freaks" are protagonists who are undercompetent enough to challenge conventional wisdom and so enable extraordinary entrepreneurial performance. In other words, freaks are "strategic" idiots. They aren't content with rational choice; they want the frenetics of irrational choice. For if you come up with a set of rules to overcome conventions and give yourself a competitive edge, you create new conventions that you either follow or sidestep, but then you're no longer a freak, you're just doing what everyone else does: orienting yourself, albeit in your own way, to accepted parameters. However, behaving "individually" isn't freakish, it's common economics. Which means that the criteria for success or failure of a freak are as vague as your economic performance. So essentially, if you take Freakonomics seriously, you will have to forget about it. No advice can be given about freaks, only taken. Analogously, there can be no useful book about idiots.

*Botcherland*—The freak factor applies today for all types of global leadership. Where the freak rules, power and power vacuum are identical. This is grotesquely evident in the fact that state apparatuses don't even take the trouble to disguise their activities—be they premeditated hos-

tilities like Russia's attack on Ukraine in 2022; be they the obvious kill-
ings of dissidents, opposition politicians, or journalists. In all cases the
state acts as if there would be no consequences, as if the deed engulfed
everything around it and had no need to defer to any kind of reality.
It befits the political choreography here that, some years before, one
of the two alleged culprits in the Russian assassination attempt on the
Russian exile Sergei Skripal bore the real name of Myshkin. The state
sends idiots because the state is an idiot, operating under a freakish
premise. Operations like these conform to the overall scheme of state
intelligence engaging in seemingly unsophisticated disinformation. A
study by the Rand Corporation speaks of a "firehose of falsehoods" in
an analysis of Russian PsyOps in the last decade or so. But this phrase
can meanwhile be applied to the metaverse of information in general.
According to Rand, apart from the classical features of propaganda—
high volume and wide distribution of messages, quick, continual,
and repeated occupation of media channels—two seemingly new approaches stand out that at first sight don't look like approaches at all:
• *the abandonment of a relationship to reality*
• *the abandonment of object consistency*
   Today a strategy might be to construct a narrative that nobody can
believe, but that is effective for this very reason. As in the above case of
Uri Geller, the failure to provide any evidence for one's claim functions
as evidence for it. It's an inversion of (Christopher) *Hitchens's razor*, according to which "what can be asserted without evidence can also be
dismissed without evidence." This new type of propaganda consists
in linking traditional methods of manipulation with dysrational approaches. This is different from the modernist propaganda model after
Bernays or Goebbels, which plays off the imperceptible against the bla-
tantly obvious, or the cheerful against the martial—at the height of
the Second World War, for example, Germany and England produced
a record number of entertainment films. This was strategic in the old
sense and the old world. Idiocratic propaganda, by contrast, functions
by means of absurdity. It's the equivalent of the espionage method of
"applied idiotics" in Thomas Pynchon's novel *Against the Day* (2006).

This method not only exhibits a "shameless willingness to disseminate partial truths or outright fictions" (Paul & Matthews); it also aims to overstrain its messaging to such a degree that a claim is convincing in its impossibility and an aim is unachievable by design. But at the same time the very existence of this "strategy" is evidence that it also encompasses the controlling instance itself. Online trolls and PsyOps agents shake hands around the world.

*Elite machines*—The truth, we remember from Kierkegaard, is recognized by absurdity, and where power claims truth it becomes recognizable by its absurdity, which falls back on itself and turns rulers into the useful idiots of their own rule. The interior of the idiocratic space has no mirrors, and strategies that claim to have outside knowledge are illusory. The reflection paradigm of power, by contrast, adheres to what the Harvard economist Shoshana Zuboff calls "instrumentarianism," that is, the myriads of data that lead like the fasces to a source of consumer control are directed by rational protagonists with the aid of rational systems, guided by rational strategies that ensure a profitable outcome.

$$Big\ Data\ +\ Elite\ =\ 1$$

In other words, power is concretized, locatable, and can be defied as such. The overall rationality of this "fascist" apparatus is unquestioned, perhaps because it beats time to the rationality of the knowledge elites, from whose educational establishments—whether liberal or conservative—international leadership is recruited. The point is that the most rigid instrumentarianism is also subject to an idiocratic imperative arising from its sheer "desire" to take effect, resulting in chaos that appears as controlling.

$$Big\ Data\ +\ Elite\ =\ 0$$

In other words, power is in a zeroed state, embodied by the new idiot. All the talk in the US about the "deep state," for example, is born out of

the subjectivation of the new idiot: the deep state supposedly has ultimate power, but for some reason it never exercises it to the full and only
does so in benign matters, as if it were an idiot that didn't know what to
do with its omnipotence. What Ernst Mach said about the universe can
also be applied to the global instrumentarium or capital itself. Capitalism seems so insurmountable because the one meaning of space also
corresponds to the one meaning of value creation. Money knows no
transcendence, the value of exchange is "divine," meaning there is no
reflection about what lies beyond it. And in essence this applies to big-
data dreams too: there is nothing to surveil because there is no distance
from anything.

*One on one*—The new idiot is the conceptual figure of this single-value,
which is spreading globally and taking on very different, also non-eco-
nomic, forms. It appears as a "tribalism," for example, that translates
the capital-one into a national-one. This kind of one-value ideology
is what unites the various nation-first principles. The Indian version
of "great again," for example, produced narratives about how ancient
India had Internet access before there was electricity, or that the invention of television goes back to traditional yoga practice. This surrealism recalls the kitsch of the post-Yugoslavian conflict, such as Serbia's
myth of the "heavenly people." These are old tunes from the new idiot.
They always play back the dialectic of incompetence: the further the
leadership departs from reality and object consistency, the "truer" its
message seems to be. One might object here that inner contradiction
is characteristic of all ideology, but this has radicalized to such a degree that its chaosmic energy is released in all directions, transforming
ideology into "idiology": self-sabotage of power as the ultimate form of
power. Zuboff calls it "radical indifference." Adorno dealt with an analogous tendency in the cultural field: "Today, when the consciousness
of rulers is beginning to coincide with the overall tendency of society,
the tension between culture and kitsch is breaking down. Culture no
longer impotently drags its despised opponent behind it, but is taking it
under its direction. [...] Nothing more exactly characterizes the condi-

tion of being at once integral and antagonistic than this incorporation of barbarity." In this respect the global administrators of the "stupid machines" (Metz & Seeßlen) are themselves no longer capable of mastering their own algorithms because they are involved in the segmentation of their system of knowledge and subject to the very devil in the details they once devised. It's the apocalyptic culmination point where everyone is befallen by everyone else's small print. Furthermore, as the highly segmentalized financial sector has shown, pro tools are too sophisticated for pro users. As one regulatory official summarized the financial crisis of 2008, the real dysfunction wasn't that the bank managements concealed things, but that they had no clue about the risks.

*It's the confidence, stupid!*—What behavioral economics has brought to light in recent decades applies equally to customer and king: "People tend to be overconfident; they display unrealistic optimism; they often deal poorly with risks; they neglect the long term" (Cass R. Sunstein). Much misjudgment can be put down to *superiority bias* or the Dunning–Kruger effect: people overrate themselves because they are unclear about their own abilities. They overestimate the control they have over their lives. They overestimate the time they have left. They overestimate their power of judgment. They overestimate their social intelligence. They overestimate their attraction. They overestimate their creditworthiness. They overestimate their competence. They overestimate how long they work. They overestimate their political commitment. They overestimate their ability to control others. And this applies to the role they adopt in a society. So entrepreneurs like to give themselves the complexion of altruists or activists—see, for example, art-sponsoring by banks, environment-sponsoring by oil companies, or the philanthropy of billionaires. A wealthy patron will underline how people are helped by his commitment, ignoring the fact that his wealth was generated at human cost. If we take Nassim Taleb's metaphor of the black swan, which stands for the occurrence of an extremely unlikely event, there is cause for alarm, since no mechanisms of "antifragility" (Taleb)—that is, of resistance against self-misjudgment and one's own shortcomings—have yet been created to deal with any future challenge. Taleb sees the reason for this primarily in the structural misinterpretation of past procedures and the related ignorance of one's own failures, which lead to a sense of entitlement: economic players believe they are due more than they actually are, that their performance is greater than it actually is, and so on. And they act accordingly. As William Davies writes, it's not just that particular individuals are exposed as corrupt or egoistic, but that established institutions begin to appear crooked. This results, according to Zygmunt Bauman, in a general collapse of trust, that is, "the belief that our leaders are not just corrupt or stupid, but inept." But the advance of incompetence has recently and ironically gone hand in hand with an increased trust in managers among employees (Edelman Trust Barometer 2019), and with an increased demand for political action from chief executives, of all people. So the decline of the politician as role model is matched by the rise of the CEO as social justice warrior.

*Top-down populism*—Modern elites have justified their authority with the virtues and knowledge of the Enlightenment. But at the same time they are responsible for the chaos they pretended to combat, referring to the incalculability of the street. For their status and solutions are part of the problem: "Elites exhibit paternal concern for their flock and protect it from its own rebellious spirit [...]. But the matter of who is to educate these pastors and by what signs we can recognize their wisdom remains rather obscure" (Jacques Rancière). To the elites—who get it from Plato—the masses appear thoroughly irrational, ignorant, malleable. They are, in the words of Edmund Burke, a "swinish multitude." In the nineteenth century they became a psychopathological given: in the context of the positivist criminology being developed by Cesare Lombroso, the precursors of Gustave Le Bon's mass psychology established the turn-of-the-century masses as a psychological corpus that was more than the sum of its parts and because of its unpredictability and propensity to violence had the general features of a manic-depressive criminal. But there was a therapy for the "delinquent masses" (as a book title from the period has them). Scientific reason came into play here, translating psychological and pharmacological findings into containment mechanisms to protect the masses from themselves and at the same time to protect itself from mass uprisings. The masses became a treatable organism, joined *en masse* by the diagnosis of manic-depressive psychosis and chloral hydrate, for example, as its tranquilizer. It's not by chance that the civilizing progress best knows how to keep Flaubert's "infinite stupidity" in check. This tendency continues in the digital age of the online giants: "They sit at the pinnacle of the division of learning, having amassed unprecedented and exclusive wealth, information, and expertise on the strength of their dispossession of our behavior" (Zuboff). At the same time this progress and wealth constantly produces the regress that oils it, as there is an epochal "ineffect" underlying the sedatives implied in all the algorithms that oppose mass unrest but whose fantastical construct of mass unrest they actually bring about. Laurent de Sutter summarizes this development as "narcocapitalism": the anesthetization of the masses, borne of scientific disciplines and disciplining, through the distribution of medicines for the treatment of mass "arousal." The anesthesia is also digital: every security update is a form of sedation, to make sure that nothing unpredictable happens. The countless security, surveillance, and control mechanisms are only an expression of the chaos cycle that now has political consequences: think of the viral spread of political bots and the difficulties social-media giants have with facing up to their social responsibility, either out of ignorance or speculation about market leadership; think of billionaires playing the world economy and instigating chaos where there should be order. One of the consequences of this is that the masses, dependent on digital or pharmacological stimuli, eventually act like drug addicts in need of their daily fix or daily leader. So it comes as no surprise that after the 2016 US presidential election a medical study discovered that "chronic use of prescription opioid drugs was correlated with support for the Republican candidate" (James S. Goodwin). Whatever our view of such studies, they point to a never-ending cycle of agitation and tranquillization: the narcotic mechanism functions as a chaosmic activator that enables profit and pacification, which cause ineffects that make profit and pacification impossible, which in turn stimulates the chaosmic activator that enables profit and pacification, which cause ineffects that make profit and pacification impossible, which in turn stimulates the chaosmic activator … and so on. Naomi Klein calls the short circuit of chaos and order "disaster capitalism." Its aim is to create frenetic subjects who need permanent sedation while being stimulated to the maximum—think of a manager overdosing on cocaine while making the deal of his life.

*Communism of capital*—Chaos, or the dialectic of incompetence it plays out, appears as "method" where capitalism loops back into its imaginary opposite. Paolo Virno has pointed out a series of ineffects of the post-Fordian economy in this regard. While Fordism was once described as the "socialism of capital" (centralization of nationalized industries, projection of the market cycle, organization of the welfare state, aim of full employment, and so on), Virno suggests calling post-Fordism the "communism of capital": "If we can say that Fordism incorporated, and rewrote in its own way, some aspects of the socialist experience, then post-Fordism has fundamentally dismissed both Keynesianism and socialism. Post-Fordism [...] puts forth [...] typical demands of communism (abolition of work, dissolution of the State, etc.). Post-Fordism is the communism of capital." The communism of capital now has two trajectories, one reactionary, the other emancipatory:

(1) The communist "withering away" of the state has become the literal program of the New Right when someone like Steve Bannon calls for the "deconstruction of the administrative state" in order to free the middle and working classes from the yoke of regulation. But most economic nationalists in recent decades have played with a variant of the "anti-bureaucratic revolution," Milošević's one-time election slogan, which doesn't lead to communism but to a right-wing populism and the liberalization and privatization of the power apparatus (from the privatization of the military, prisons, and healthcare to the accumulation of media power). This development is driven by a "fetishistic cult of differences" (Virno) that can and does evolve into armed conflict.

(2) This fetishistic cult paradoxically stands for an emancipatory version of the communism of capital as represented, for example, by tech visionaries: Ray Kurzweil, Aaron Bastani, and others expect the communist society to be brought about by a twenty-something-century technological revolution, enabled by low production costs, a surfeit of production assets, free entrepreneurship, and open-source practices. Robots are the communists of the future, and companies are the future societies. The dynamic of information technology is an important driver of this kind of "fully automated luxury communism" (Bastani), as the development has accelerated exponentially since the late nineteenth century. It wasn't even restrained by the two world wars, as Kurzweil emphasizes, and is already impacting social organization: "This sort of collective decision-making today, is never forced, it's spontaneous, people coming together to share and build on each other's ideas." Google pioneer Larry Page also observes the rise of new collectives: "The societal goal is our primary goal," and "we need revolutionary change" driven by new technologies. Like an original communist, Page propagates the abolition of wage labor, which will soon be replaced by robots and AI. "Change tends to be revolutionary, not evolutionary" (Page). He is not alone among tech giants with his overcoming of labor and state and resulting realization of the Marxist admin paradise, which he would naturally expect to lead. And who wouldn't like to become the boss of communism? If you enter "revolution" and an IT name in the search engine, something sensible usually comes out. In short, the communism of capital has two completely different future trajectories—the cult of irrational flesh and the cult of the rational machine—which are both "ineffective" in as much as they occur simultaneously. This is perhaps why the automated revolution hasn't happened yet, and why, for example, in twenty-first-century Ukraine twentieth-century armies are conducting nineteenth-century national warfare. The future, any future, is yet to come.

*Short circuits*—The age of the idiot, so it appears, is accompanied by the "age of the scam," bolstered by the "age of entropy" (Streeck), the digital age, the "nihilistic age" (Rancière), the age of monopolies, the media age, or the "age of surveillance capitalism" (Zuboff). It's an age swamped with ages—in the sense of Paul Valéry's *tot capita tot tempora*. Comparable with the ideology critique of the 1960s or the postmodernism debates of the 1980s, with their focus on the libidinous structures of capitalism and its wish-machines, today's diagnoses revolve around the dysfunction of political institutions in the "post-democracy" (Rancière) or "post-politics" (Mouffe & Žižek). The basis here is the levelling out of the contradiction between labor and capital, post-ideological all-in-one parties, apolitical rituals of consensus in a democracy without demos, along with the blurring of expertise and dilettantism (blogger versus journalists, entrepreneurs versus career politicians, and so on), accompanied by new "radical technologies" (Adam Greenfield) that are increasingly colonizing our everyday lives—smartphones, drones, self-driving cars, home assistants, blockchain technology, augmented-reality, and everything AI. The emancipatory and regressive aspects of this "age of the idiot," as I call it, interpenetrate. It's as much of an advantage to society that "any idiot" can become president as it's a disadvantage that "an idiot" actually becomes president. It's as much of an advantage for every user to be able to comment unfiltered as it's a disadvantage for them to actually do so. It's as much of an advantage as a disadvantage to have "individualists" as colleagues. It's as much of an advantage as a disadvantage to "bring fresh air" as an outsider. It's as much of an advantage for the private to become political as it's a disadvantage when the private becomes political.

*Total significance*—Idiocracy, in which universal reason annuls itself voluntarily, goes beyond the competence of individuals. It isn't so easy, even for the most sophisticated among us, to state exactly what we stand for and what we want without contradicting ourselves. "Liberal" can be used as an insult or felt as a value, even by one and the same person—if it's meant economically here and ethically there, for example, or on the one hand politically, on the other programmatically in the sense of the "freedom of dissenters." And it's now possible to imagine an argument in which blurred concepts and fragments of thought attain total significance. In an idiocracy we argue past one another, not with one another. George Orwell saw this coming: "The words democracy, socialism, freedom, patriotic, realistic, justice, have each of them several different meanings which cannot be reconciled with one another. [...] Words of this kind are often used in a consciously dishonest way. That is, the person who uses them has his own private definition, but allows his hearer to think he means something quite different." The difference today lies in the fact that words aren't always used in a consciously dishonest way, but rather like reused leftovers from an unfinished debate. The ideal of the Socratic dialogue between mutually edifying individuals has disappeared beyond the second realm of the idiot and into the abyss beyond the edge of the earth. If the earth is a sphere, we'll see each other again. If not, then the earth is flat after all.

*Culture of denial*—The new idiot doesn't doubt, he *denies*. He doesn't wish to expose the ground of being, rather to elevate the groundlessness of the paradigm of thought. He calls this groundlessness "truth." The welcome democratization of the outsider status goes along with the international sabotage of knowledge, which has brought about something like a "conspiracy industry." In recent decades genocide denial, for example, was a matter of clandestine groups, or it was part of the national ideology, as in Iran in relation to the Holocaust or in Turkey regarding the Armenians. There is no grand annual ceremonial remembrance of the massacred indigenous population of the United States either. What's new is the emergence of denier networks through the online distribution of political imaginaries, and the provision of the necessary ideological backup to clandestine groups by a "denialist mainstream." This can be seen, for example, in the alt-right movement, whose anti-Semitism became acceptable to the conservative mainstream through Trumpist Islamophobia. So now you can have devoted evangelical supporters of Israel babbling simultaneously about the clandestine worldwide influence of George Soros and "Rothschild capital." The same logic applies to the "climate deniers," whose idiocratic motto seems to be "better wrong now than alive in future." Decades before the dawn of the Internet, Adorno discerned an epidemic danger in these dynamics of adjustment: "The bottomless solitude of the deluded has a tendency to collectivization and so quotes the delusion into existence. This pathic mechanism harmonizes with the social one prevalent today, whereby those socialized into desperate isolation hunger for community and flock together in cold mobs. So folly becomes an epidemic: insane sects grow with the same rhythm as big organizations." Denialism isn't a matter of stupidity, psychosis, or propaganda. It's more of a post-Enlightenment state of groundlessness. We are destroying the foundations of thinking until being right is all we are—even if we're wrong. "To be in denial is to know at some level. To be a denialist is to never have to know at all" (Keith Kahn-Harris).

*Tinkling facts*—What ineffects teach us is not that the lie is en vogue, but that access to competence and incompetence, truth and untruth is blocked, and that the ability to be both competent and incompetent, both authentic and false, has political consequences: whoever breaks through the blockade of meaning first is right. Donald Trump said that the voice on the infamous "pussy-grabber" recording wasn't his *after* having apologized for his statements on it. This sequence of events is idiocritically relevant. That fact that various instances of idiotic behavior recurrently appear in the media shows that information death has become as representable as the heat death of the universe. An end state in which absolutely nothing makes sense any more, in which the absurd is real and the real absurd, to put it in Hegelian terms. The death of information is an inherent "rational" state in which a message is pushed from one corner of the single consciousness to another for no reason. Meanings are shifted with no sense of linguistic play, while the will to absurdity stimulates a general talkativeness the sooner to bring on its own end. The question of idiocracy is recurrently one of apocalyptic groundlessness.

*Poetry & bullshit*—This groundlessness is at the heart of the post-truth society. If, in *The Trial* (1925), Franz Kafka writes that "correct understanding of something and misunderstanding of the same thing are not entirely mutually exclusive," today's online and offline trolls take this as a mandate. They create confusion where in fact none is possible, and their sole benefit is the destruction of discourse and the creation of pseudo-discourse, pseudo-politics, pseudo-states, and pseudo-history. In his essay *On Bullshit* (2005), Harry G. Frankfurt claims that while the liar accepts a truth value so as to distract from it by lying, the bullshit actor recognizes no such value. Facts and fantasies lie on the shelf before him and he helps himself at random, depending on the formulations his claims require. Frankfurt writes that bullshit is more dangerous to truth than the lie, "for the essence of bullshit is not that it is *false* but that it is *phony.*" Not by chance has there been a "bullshit-job boom" in recent years (Nathan Heller). According to David Graeber, people with bullshit jobs are an unproductive workforce existing alongside the class of productive workers. When a machine turns a worker into the supervisor of a machine, and in a next step this supervision is replaced by AI, what remains in the end is the mere representation of the production process in the form of pseudo-work. At the end of the expressionless movement of a production robot there is the zero expression of the worker pretending to control this process. Analogously to the bullshit discourse, the bullshit labor market blurs the distinction between productivity and unproductivity. Pretending to work is equivalent to working, and working life is populated by posers. We all spend our lives in an interim, always "busy," yet accomplishing essentially nothing. The bullshit protagonist is a practical consequence of the new idiot, who interweaves his fast-food freedom with unrecognized artistic freedom. Hence the term "bullshit artist." But the artistic appellation is misleading where there is no "imaginative play." There's good and bad art in the bullshit world too.

*Totalities*—Idiocracy defeats clarity by means of clarity. In this sense, for Hannah Arendt, the ideal subjects of totalitarian rule are post-factual: subjects for whom all facts are "alternative." George Orwell once said that political language makes "lies sound truthful" and gives "an appearance of solidity to pure wind." Idiocratic discourse, however, is able to break this distinction and present the windy and the solid as two options of one and the same circumstance, and thus to declare the arbitrary as the highest expression of the will to absurdity. Curiously, the arts, too, are a permanent challenge to the distinction between fact and fiction, without becoming the subject of a totalitarian regime but also without questioning the totality itself. The para-factual world of art differs from the post-factual in that it sees its utopias as already realized. "Homer makes lies seem so real that they enter the world and walk among us," says Lewis Hyde. Art proposes a real-existing parallel society, where it makes itself at home. But in a post-factual world the sense of reality and the sense of possibility are interwoven. Post-factual protagonists don't shape the things to come, but dwell in the impossible; there is no liberating effect. Yet they are nonetheless creative in bringing about new forms of obscuration. This post-factual creativity, be it derp face, silly diatribe, or TikTok video, is difficult to grasp. The idiocratic mind usurps the disciplines and inflates the online signifiers as an end in itself. The post-factual actor aims at indeterminacy and the imponderable. Or as Arron Banks, founder of the British Leave.EU campaign, once put it: "Facts don't work." He should have added: "Possibilities don't work either." If you're not good at anything, all you have to do is *whatever*.

*Somewhere or other*—According to George Eliot, an idiot is someone who expects things to happen that can't. For Adorno the Hegelian contradiction of fact and counterfact is non-identical in regard to identity. Contradiction and identity are "welded together." Fact and counterfact are related, as theists and atheists are related as to the concept of God. Fact and post-fact, however, have no shared basis, only shares of fate. Chantal Mouffe refers to this when she distinguishes agonism from antagonism: either a conflict has a jointly identified basis, or each of the disputing parties brings their own definition to the confrontation. The contest will then take place off the playing field, as with a conflict whose rules aren't recognized by either side and therefore lasts longer than a declared war. A post-factual conflict exists today, for example, when one party attacks some object that it identifies as a representative of the enemy, and this enemy "discovers" the representation of its identity through the attack. Today any idiot can become the proverbial terrorist by destroying something or other somewhere or other in the world and shouting something or other. In an idiocracy, a freak accident is a deliberate act.

*Politics of thought*—Idiocracy ensures both the spread of incompetence and a fragmented politics of thought. "The idiot heard the sounds, but they had no meaning for him. He lived inside somewhere, apart, and the little link between word and significance hung broken" (Theodore Sturgeon). Life is stuck in the accepted, if unconnected meaning-stimuli of its surroundings, and its meme generators stimulate market value and regulate political, social, or cultural commitment. Such communications are "strictly meaningless, in the sense that they not only do not point to any discoverable object, but are hardly even expected to do so" (Orwell). Idiocrats are satisfied with this state of affairs, in which individuals convincingly represent non-existent positions, typically with a derp smile on their faces. The new idiot disappears behind his narrative, like a Shakespearian jester, always considering himself above it. You might ignore the discursive spectacle, but what Adorno predicted in his *Minima Moralia* still applies: "There is nothing innocuous left." The post-fact creates the reality it comfortably denies. The cartoonist Georges Wolinski, who was murdered in the jihadist attack on *Charlie Hebdo* in 2015, once wrote: "Paradise is full of idiots who believe it exists."

## THE FRENETIC SUBJECT

*Inflammation*—The self-politics of the new idiot brings about a subject "inflamed" by its own being, continually doing something, wanting something, starting or stopping something without being able to free itself from this state. "We're dying to be ourselves," twitters Kanye West before sitting on President Ubu's lap in the Oval Office to bluster on camera about alternative universes, dragon energies, and oxygen-powered airplanes. This spectacle of the ego is an echo of what Eva Illouz once called "the making of an intensely specialized emotional culture," or what appears in Lauren de Sutter as "a regime of intensity challenging the way in which being orientates itself so that it can be qualified as sane." Frenetic self-performance can be as much an expression of boredom, apathy, or exhaustion as of creativity, alertness, or vitality. If we're tired, we're *dead* tired, if nice, then *super* nice, if party, then *badass*, if career, then *stellar*, if exhausted, then *burnout*, if child, then *gifted*, if partner, then *understanding*, if hobbies, then *lots*, if free, then *libertine*, if noise, then *affray*, if problem, then *crisis* … The word frenetic goes back to *phrenitis* (Gr. φρήν *phrēn*, for "spirit," "soul"), an antique term for a feverish mental illness. This feverishness distinguishes the new idiot from the old. The more frenetic the subject, the quicker it is exhausted in media procedures, the more self-referential its desires, and the more opaque its relationship to the world. Alain Ehrenberg speaks of "the perfect disorder of the democratic human being" that reveals a "sovereignty of the self," but this is an aspect of freneticism that appears in the modish diagnosis of depression: the "weariness of the self" (*fatigue d'être soi*) is the result of an inflammation. The aim of the freneticism is to "mobilize as much of one's potential as possible and to help it unfold" (Reckwitz). This is a type of idiot "that has totally interiorized the dynamic of capital" (Camatte). "Condemned to lifelong apprenticeship, to flexibility, to the reign of the short term, he must embrace his condition as a soluble, fungible subject to be able to respond to what is constantly demanded of him: to become another" (Mbembe). Freneticism, seen in this way, is the expression of a systematic abandonment in which capital makes an example of the individual.

*Culture freaks*—Frenetic individuals, once exposed to the public, are no menace to the public because they are marked as freaks—think of talkshow arenas in which hapless guests expose their privacy or fight each other in front of a cynical TV audience. But, as we have seen, freaks are also at the core of economic optimization; they are "different" for the benefit of systemic performance. Whatever the "freakishness" of a situation, all non-freaks believe themselves in the safe space of an imaginary center, where "repressive tolerance" (Marcuse) alternates with tolerated repression. The freak is both a problem bearer and component of a frenetic culture of showcasing. All idiosyncrasy appears as the packaging of a frenetic pseudo-individualism that while it remains within the bounds of normality foils any outsider attempt to find a political voice; that is, it not only changes economic practices but also the economy itself. The zeroed society is the rumbling deep from which something is continually rising—monsters or minions. The desiring-machines of singularized society are the apparatuses that vary, intensify, and control the mass idiotization of virtual arousal. This also explains the ritualized production of stars, which is nothing other than the frenetic expression of a sequence of zeros. While every real idiosyncrasy is consistently leveled, at the same time "any idiot" can become a star.

*Undaily madness*—"It makes me incredibly sad," says Martin Page's Antoine, who sets out to become an idiot, "to know that we're not free, and that even each conscious thought or act is made at the cost of a wound that will never heal." Public idiotization is based on following procedure:

- Wherever single "idiots" appear in the public, they are abandoned to the spectacle of the many idiots (*wound*)
- Idiots realize their potential by exposing themselves to the gaze of others without ever finding themselves (*absurdity*)
- This exposure is itself injurious, that is, the spectacle sabotages itself (*idiocy*)

The procedure ensures the ubiquity of idiotization, and the freneticism ensures the procedure. For as soon as they leave their privileged "safe spaces" (TV station, villa, club, and so on), even the biggest cynic becomes a useful idiot. The financial elites digging bunkers for the coming "ecocalypse" forget that idiotization is making survivalists or "preppers" of everyone, that the elites themselves are booty without knowing it, and that their self-imposed isolation will become the problem they thought was the solution. It won't be some saboteur who cuts off their air supply in the end; they will do it themselves. A first madness made them dig the bunker; a second will destroy it.

*All the more useful, like it or not*—Frenetic subjects come about when systemic burdens are transferred to individuals, who are unable to carry them but do so anyway. You become a part of the pattern whose usefulness outdoes the objectives. It's what happens with the so-called "useful idiot." Never mind Lenin's supposedly first application of the term, if I go shopping and walk around town with a printed grocery bag, I'm advertising the company I chose without being paid to do so. So if I want to regain control over the situation and turn the bag inside out to hide the logo, for example, the salespeople will look at me in surprise and take me for an idiot, although I've just de-idiotized myself. Freneticists, on the other hand, want the opposite, namely for everyone in town to see where they go shopping, even though they get nothing from it personally (which is kind of the point). It's also comparable with myriads of voluntary content providers, aka "users," who happily keep the social-media giants afloat. For the freneticist, every market segment is also a community that needs their understanding and to which they wish to belong, even though—in essence—they are no longer required as individuals; rather, their idiosyncrasy is payed out infinitely. Freneticists play their part in viral marketing for a pittance; they turn the product into a lifestyle and any lifestyle into a product when they, say, gain online fame as influencers. Every increase in brazenness comes with increased productivity. Freneticists, in this sense, are "engulfed by a mysterious activity that bears all the features of commercial life without there being actually any business to transact" (Adorno). They want to become all the more useful in an already utilitarian world.

*Idiotic loops*—The new bursts in and asserts its usefulness, and so becomes the benchmark of usefulness. The new idiot chooses the new as if it were the old. Compared with the old usefulness, the new usefulness is phase-shifted, as increasingly shorter product cycles make clear. While consumer electronics used to last for decades, nowadays more complicated gizmos that often don't live up to their claims are offered in rapid succession. New usefulnesses catapult consumers into new idiotic procedures. The vendors' aim is "a closed loop that feeds on, reinforces, and amplifies the individual user's inclination toward fusion with the group and the tendency to over-share personal information" (Zuboff). The loop objectivizes desire: "Capital generates needs of its own; mistakenly, we perceive these needs as if they belonged to us. [...] We are being expelled from the sphere of lived immanence – where life relates to life instead of subjugating itself to external ends" (Han). But external ends and lived immanence are two aspects of one and the same frenetic subject. Resistance to desire is part of desire or is desire itself. "The stupid thing is not outside me but rather with me: in me. [...] The thing's depth of use [...] is precisely the abyss that so unfathomably stares back the longer one looks into it. [...] The user interface turns me into an idiot; the depth of use is sheer exasperation" (Metz & Seeßlen). The frenetic subject lives out the paradox of the consumerist condition: exasperated and happy, powerless and free.

*Compulsory freedom*—An idiotized person is the structural residue of economic, aesthetic, or political decisions made without his or her assistance. At the same time the idiot is continually doing something, as if he or she were able to influence these decisions. According to Adorno, "The subjugation of life to the process of production imposes as a humiliation on everyone something of the isolation and solitude that we are tempted to regard as resulting from our own superior choice." This has given rise to a wellness ideology focused on individual coping strategies, a "lonely struggle to survive," as Laurie Penny describes it, or as Ken Loach depicts it in I, DANIEL BLAKE (2016). The film follows an unemployed man in his struggle against his compulsory idiotization, by which the authorities force him into bureaucratic legal disputes he can't win. It's a capitalist catch 22 for the unfit: although Blake has a heart condition, he wants to work, but he is required to apply for unemployment benefit. The fact that he is able to make the application proves his fitness for work, however. But he has a heart condition and is unfit for work, so he has to apply for unemployment benefit ... In the end it turns out that he can only receive a certificate of employment once he's dead. In the protagonist's heart attack the film reproduces an absurd catharsis of the job market: in the "perfect" welfare state every unemployed person is dead and therefore relieves the burden on the system. While alive they can be systematically harassed. What Richard Sennett once called the "infantilisation of the workers" can be more fundamentally described as the frenetic structuring of contemporary life, as the "consequence of a system that prevents people from thinking independently and that fails to treat employees as adults" (Paul Verhaeghe). However, Loach also shows his protagonist making his individuation process public with a graffiti action, thus politicizing his case. "I, Daniel Blake" becomes an inscription on a public building. It's a "Thompsonizing" gesture, but turned around ideologically. The frenetic subject is driven on the one hand into the pool of the nameless, but on the other he becomes an existential activist, quite literally, *in his own name.*

*Gothamists*—Zygmunt Bauman once introduced the figures of the flâneur, vagabond, tourist, and gambler to outline some late-modern ways of life. The qualities of non-commitment, freedom, mobility, and adventurousness these figures represent can be united in the frenetic tourist, who fulfils all requirements of "flexible identity" (Bauman). This type of idiot is inflamed by his or her surroundings. Tourists discover and apply new technologies for their "specialty"; they open up new destinations, turn this into a business, found associations or operate politically, if you bring to mind the holiday pilgrims who gather every year in Mussolini's birthplace. This para-avant-garde acts in cross-cultural and multidisciplinary ways, even advancing into warzones. The adventurers want to prove something to themselves and to others as if their lives depended on it. And sometimes their lives do depend on it, given the numerous deaths of amateur mountaineers on Everest. What used to be considered the province of extreme athletes has given way to mass tourism. Therefore it isn't by chance that the term "idiot" is used in connection with vacationers who desecrate holy places, litter beaches, or destroy natural habitats while leaving remnants of their petit bourgeois life behind. This ranges from the spontaneous private porno at the foot of an Egyptian pyramid, to "balconing"—a favorite discipline in Spanish resorts involving drunken jumping from balconies into hotel pools—to camera drones crashing into Milan Cathedral, to other forms of civilized vandalism. Since the 1950s psychologists have also spoken of the "neurotic paradox," a form of destructive behavior that seeks a short-term reward even at the cost of negative long-term effects. This corresponds to the dialectic insight that tourist fundamentalism ruins the destinations that make it possible, as in the case of the millions of lovers whose symbolic padlocks cause the collapse of the bridges to which they were attached—or as one article put it, "love is destroying infrastructure." "All the normal processes are suppressed in order to arrive directly at the imposition of what is desired," writes Ortega y Gasset about "the mass-man." But today's "mass" is all of us. Reward-seeking and desire-fulfilling are connected to the burden of late-modern restlessness. Due to a lack of goals, present stimuli multiply, with the ersatz goal of "desires that give rise to new desires the moment they are fulfilled" (Streeck). This at least explains the long lines to the summit.

*Selfie-made*—From the end perspective media freneticism turns us all into tourists in our own lives, which expire as they are experienced. The worldwide increase in fatal selfie accidents is the result of something like a metaphysical discipline. It is perhaps the most intimate form of self-sabotage driven by new technology, and is causing alarm among the authorities, who issue official warnings about selfie-related dangers. In 2015 the Russian Ministry of the Interior, for example, published a brochure illustrating suicidal situations (excerpt):

When Walter C. Parker writes that an idiot is self-refuting because he or she doesn't know that privacy and individual autonomy entirely depend on community, then such deliberately undeliberate suicidal acts, often nominated for the "Darwin Award," represent an absurd fulfilment of the idea of community. Such a death lets everybody else know that we're all equal. The new idiot permanently suspends the difference between self and world; he or she is driven like a one-day wonder by "Moment," which according to Henri Lefebvre represents the "attempt to achieve the total realization of a possibility." The frenetic subject thus constantly feeds energy into the projections and projectiles of the contemporary world. It "pumps up" any given moment to make it seem more than it really is. An idea that propagates a plus by expanding the surrounding space. In 2014 Apple's iPhone 6 was advertised as being "bigger than bigger," that is, size was no longer conceived as discrete but as an absolute relation, as a general plus that imaginatively exceeds infinity—more infinite than infinite. It wasn't the gadgets that expanded in size, but the space they defined. The present is bursting its bounds.

*Superfluous*—It's difficult to accept that modern life no longer has anything to do with oneself. "If yesterday's drama of the subject was exploitation by capital, the tragedy of the multitude today is that they are unable to be exploited at all. They are abandoned subjects, relegated to the role of a 'superfluous humanity.' Capital hardly needs them anymore to function" (Mbembe). In *The Culture of the New Capitalism* (2006) Richard Sennett points to an increasing sense of the meaninglessness and futility of work resulting from the requirements of the worldwide labor market, automatization, and how society copes with the ageing process. In the first case this leads to ostracism and resentment by the respective "regular workforce," whose redundancy is mirrored in an influx of migrants. In the second and third cases technological and demographic developments lead to the exclusion of formerly meaningful occupations. What the identity theorist Erik Erikson once wrote about changes in ego psychology applies all too well to today's frenetic subjects: "The patient of today suffers most under the problem of what he should believe in and who he should – or, indeed, might – be or become; while the patient of early psychoanalysis suffered most under inhibitions which prevented him from being what and he thought he knew he was." The freneticist basically has to do with not existing without an avatar. Frenetic subjects—whether star freak, politico freak, or freakonomist—have to thematize, mobilize, and reconfigure themselves in order to exist. There is a dominant fear of indifference, not of the void. Worse than death, writes Fernando Pessoa in the *Book of Disquiet*, is never to have existed.

## WENDY'S WORLD

*They're not thinking straight!*
Wendy

*Visions*—We are surrounded by visions, but it's difficult to distinguish visions from inflationary images. Almost every technological product is now marketed as visionary, modeling the future into a sales scheme and reproducing insignia of progress. Sci-fi films reduce materiality, becoming cleaner, brighter, airier, more minimal the more futurey they pretend to be—except when they're dystopian, then steampunk dominates and the dust drifts down from the ceiling. In the clean Silicon Valley time to come, control panels become projections, screens become holograms, and people become androids. Future presents are continually being predicted, from the weather forecast to the election promise, from the program note to the opinion poll. But a vision is something different from a prediction of future events. A vision is the future image of an event *that has already occurred.*

*The hole*—An ad by the fast-food chain Wendy's (2013) depicts a world situation that will either never occur or is already with us. At the beginning of the film we see a plain on which a circular hole is gaping. People run up, jump in, and disappear into it in an endless stream. They don't appear to be in panic or confused; things seem to be going as they should. In the middle of the crowd a guy with a Pippi Longstocking wig stands out: it's Wendy. Wendy begins to mistrust the situation. Says Wendy: "Hey, something's not right here. It feels a little creepy. They're not thinking straight!" It dawns on Wendy: "A hamburger that sits around in a warming tray?" Wendy now grumbles about how crispy a hamburger has to be grilled, but it won't stay crispy if it's kept warm for too long because then the meat would get too dry. As Wendy utters her fast-food wisdom, other runners begin to notice her. She encourages them to turn away from the hole and run in a different direction, towards the world of crispy hamburgers. More and more runners join Wendy, thus disrupting the main stream. At the height of the revolution, Wendy's burger is blended in and a slogan appears: "Wendy's. Made to Order." — Now let's imagine the ad world was real: the hole would be a kind of modern totem, guiding all our ideas about the world. Generation after generation of hole runners would define themselves in its terms; children would be told bedtime stories about the hole; it would be mentioned in the Holey Bible. Jesus wouldn't have been crucified but holed. Everything would be holey. Every desire, every story would be full of holes and would begin with "One day …" and end with "… in the hole." Such a attractor is comparable with the leitmotif of the sci-fi flic THE ISLAND (2005). The inhabitants of an isolated colony live in hope of coming to the island of their dreams as a reward for their life's work. In reality they are clones, financed by wealthy clients for their organs. Unlike the protagonists of THE ISLAND or LOGAN'S RUN (1976), the thought of liberation never occurs to Wendy. At first it looks as if she's questioning the planetary determination of the hole ("They're not thinking straight!"), but the first thing that occurs to this "revolutionary" is only a better version of the same product. Wendy doesn't refer to the absurdity of there being a hole that everybody is jumping into, but continues to talk about fast food. Her new deal is a *New Deal!* So Wendy and her burger-garde will dig a new hole for new followers to jump into. The idiosyncratic redhead has dissolved completely into the product scheme—in fact her idiosyncrasy is just another brand. The ever-present demise of all is never at issue while the continuous stream of runners ensures the natural course of things.

*A bunch of idiots*—Traditional figurations of the idiot type of the first-order occupy the position of the outsider, of the inner emigration that enables them to see the world as it is, while today's complacent consumers aren't outsiders but disposable flâneurs on the promenades of late capitalism. So you might think that such conformists are the opposite of idiots, as Byung-Chul Han says: "Today, it seems, the type of the outsider – the idiot, the fool – has all but vanished from society. Thoroughgoing digital networking and communication have massively amplified the compulsion to conform. The attendant violence of consensus is suppressing idiotisms." This is true, but only if you take one idiot type and assume that the conforming procedures aren't idiotizing in themselves. In this sense the new idiot is the contemporary *zoon paradoxon*, whose uniqueness and universality imbue the many. In *The Weariness of the Self* (2004) Alain Ehrenberg shows how in today's societies everyone is called on to be unique. He writes about a "democratization of the exceptional." The particular self and the general self are both incommensurable and identical, are unrelated and yet share the syllable "I." The Is are drawn to the same hole, the attractor that embodies the law of value that leads all people to the same "life goal": you run towards something all your life, only to find out that the actual meaning of life doesn't lie in the goal but in this running that you've done all your life. Idiotism can be understood here as an auto-poietic leveling, that is, the adjustment of everyone to everyone else in a generalizing process. In the trajectory of Wendy's world everyone is individual in the same way, happy in the same way, unhappy in the same way, dies in the same way, will have lived, drunk, partied, laughed in the same way as the generic individual of a mindless fortune.

*Planetarism*—Martin Heidegger also discusses idiotism as a global phenomenon of the simultaneity of difference and indifference: "'Idi-otism' is not meant as a psychiatric definition of mental and emotional obtuseness, but rather as that historical state in which everyone, every-where, and at all times, identifies his ιδιον—that which is his own—as the same as that of everyone else, and pursues it either intentionally or unwittingly. Idiotism is the being-historical essence of the They." Heidegger links this idiotism to what he calls "planetarism," which re-fers to the global human responsibility to the anonymous totality of ev-eryday life, the "abandonment of beings by being." In this context Avi-tal Ronell has pointed out that Robert Musil contrived his man without qualities at more or less the same time as Martin Heidegger his figure of thought "the They" ("man" in German). Together they could have written the *They Without Qualities*, which would be a good descrip-tion of the planetary determination of idiotism. The They expresses the indiscrimination of the modern world in relation to the actuality of existence, from which what is one's own emerges as respectively mine and that of everyone else, as Heidegger emphasizes: "Idiotism means shifting that which is one's own to that which belongs to everyone. [...] One even finds oneself in the own that is everyone's." In idiotism Hei-degger sees an "essential confinement to the worldly," accompanied by a nimble lack of consciousness, an agile idiocy: "Idiotsim is [...] not | peculiar to 'idiots' (that is, people of limited aptitude). On the contrary, idiotism includes the craftiness and agility and ingenuity of the historically technical human being. [...] It is not enough for there to be an apparatus on every floor of every building. Every "family member," the servants, the children must each have their own appliance, so as to be able to be everyone, quickly and easily to know and to hear and to "be" what everyone else also is." Not by chance does Heidegger also call planetarism "Americanism," the "death of modernity | in ruin." Alexis de Tocqueville saw a precursor of this constellation in 1840 in his work on American democracy, calling it a new form of tyranny: "The first thing that strikes the observation is an innumerable multitude of men all equal and alike, incessantly endeavoring to procure the petty and paltry pleasures with which they glut their lives. Each of them, living apart, is as a stranger to the fate of all the rest [...] he touches them, but he feels them not; he exists but in himself and for himself alone." The trajectory of power, which is both sweeping and inconspicuous ("absolute, minute, regular, provident, and mild"), that is, a "democratic despotism," an "inverted totalitarianism" (Sheldon Wolin), extends through industrial modernity as a leveling energy. It can be seen today in public communication: "Dimmed to a tolerable atmosphere [...], a firm, pebble-like politeness of mutually coordinated speech forms, to shield each of us from his own (more focused) awareness" (Botho Strauß). In *The Society of Spectacle* (1967) Guy Debord writes that "the images which detached themselves from every aspect of life fuse in a common stream where the unity of life can no longer be reestablished" and that "the spectacle in general, as the concrete inversion of life, is the autonomous movement of the non-living." In other words, reality unfolds into a new generality, the great attractor-hole of all of its moments. Subjects, images, and life are decoupled, proceed individually as virtual points in time, much like data bits. Their meanings are as varied as they are indeterminate; their origin is "the loss of the unity of the world, and the gigantic expansion of the modern spectacle expresses the totality of this loss. [...] What ties the spectators together is no more than an irreversible relation at the very center which maintains their isolation" (Debord). This is emblematically demonstrated in a scene in Steven Soderbergh's SCHIZOPOLIS (1996), in which interpersonal communication only occurs descriptively, and the general is imposed on the particular:

> *Fletcher*: Generic greeting.
> *Wife*: Generic greeting returned.
> *Fletcher*: Imminent sustenance ...
> *Wife*: Overly dramatic ... statement regarding upcoming meal.
> *Fletcher*: Ooh. False reaction indicating hunger and excitement.

While this dialogue works as a metadiscourse referencing interpersonal exchange, the idiocratic condition has to be imagined as if we had learned no other way of speaking. What kind of humans would this make us? Would we live our lives for no other reason than a general reason?

*Homo stans & homo mutans*—As Herbert Marcuse observed in the 1960s, linear explanations of exploitation and alienation fall too short "when the individuals identify themselves with the existence which is imposed upon them and have in it their own development and satisfaction." In this self-deception Marcuse sees the ascent of "one-dimensional man": "The products [...] promote a false consciousness which is immune against its falsehood. [...] Thus emerges a pattern of one-dimensional thought and behavior in which ideas, aspirations, and objectives that, by their content, transcend the established universe of discourse and action are either repelled or reduced to terms of this universe." Half a century later and this experience of the world is inherent in post-industrial society living through a permanent crisis of self-realization. In the 1970s Pier Paolo Pasolini spoke of the "anthropological mutation" or "anthropological revolution" to refer to the structural narrowing of homo economicus into homogenized individuals. This mutation, described by Roland Barthes as cultural homogenization, amounts to a social paradigm that redraws the stress zones of social existence. As Adorno noted in *Minima Moralia* (1951), the bourgeois principle "has passed from the objectivity of the social process into the composition of its colliding and jostling atoms, and therewith as if into anthropology." The anthropological transformations are ubiquitous. A socio-cognitive leveling can be seen, for example, in the way our media-savvy public life flattens out content almost beyond recognition by making it "over-recognizable." Non-fiction, sales talk, lectures, or online commentaries, no matter how individual they pretend to be, can increasingly be reduced to a single linguistic type. Social bots will take on the dialogue function at some point, and descriptive algorithms will end up talking to themselves in the end, as in Jacques Camatte's dystopian view of "the transformation of the mind into a computer which can be programmed by the laws of capital." A completely programmed, ascertained human being, *homo stans*, as the result of the changing human being, *homo mutans*—that would be the highest stage of idiotism and the beginning of an inverted Turing test, consisting in asking how an artificial intelligence could convince a natural intelligence of its artificiality. We already speak artificially in order to appear to our advantage in professional relations, adapting ourselves to the second nature of social life. The most artificial of all intelligences is both an anthropologically mutating "madness of economic reason" (David Harvey) and the realization of what Franco Berardi called the "neuro-totalitarian system," in which all wishes are fulfilled "but human beings cannot find themselves and enjoyment continually lies in the future" (Camatte).

*Zombie and time*—Heidegger's planetary rule of the They suggests a generic enframing that manifests as capitalist totality. Pop-cultural representations give us the clone or the zombie as its corresponding idiot types. Clones—here popularly understood as the technological reproduction of humans without a "soul"—embody a techno-utopian and zombies a post-apocalyptic attack on individuation. Clones, androids, cyborgs, and so on, are "homegrown" humanoids. They don't become of their own accord. For them what we call personality, soul, or consciousness is a threshold experience, as played through in the sci-fi genre. STAR TREK's Data, for example, recurrently discovers human feelings or shows them without having them. Zombies aren't individual either but neither do they form zombie communities, which is why they are a metaphor for acephalous consumerism when they wander around the malls in DAWN OF THE DEAD (1978), for example. The undead may act jointly but they do so alone. Zombies and clones are so notorious as film figures because they are humanoid without being human, because they reveal the reality of the double: something about them corresponds to something in us, and this is precisely what Adorno refers to as typical of capitalist totality, "the subject's transition to a passive, atomistic, reflex-type conduct." Today we could call this—in Hegelian inversion—*happy unconsciousness*, as subjective happiness is no longer a matter of awareness and has to be dragged to the surface with all symbolic force. Jordan Peele's Us (2019) has given the most recent commentary on this permanent unhinging of the bourgeois idyll. It joins the happy unconsciousness with the symbolism of the charity event *Hands Across America* (1986) into a dastardly end-time plot. This story confronts the identity of every human family with their really existing underworld variants—the zombie-like "tethered" subsisting underground in the sewers. These creatures feel their time has come and are pushing to the civilized surface to kill their parallel families. It's a deadly doppelgänger motif that alludes to social and racial issues in the United States and emphasizes the morbidity of the American Dream. Bret Easton Ellis's *American Psycho* did this for the 1980s, but the scope of Us is broader. When at the end of the film the underworld dwellers hold hands across America, it suddenly becomes clear that the antithesis of US society has broken its ideological commitment to the pursuit of happiness—as an opposite in itself.

*Hunkering down*— Marx's notion of (bourgeois) idiotism occupies the opposite pole of the generic idiocy of the many outlined above, for the bourgeoisie, who emulate the idiot type of the greedy millionaire (today's billionaire), aren't concerned with the planetary whole but with their private piece of it, eventually encompassing the entire world. Referring here also to his concept of the blinkered specialist, or *Fachidiot* in

German, Marx implies a subject antipole: a total differentiation of each person in his/her uniqueness as a private individual, as furthered by the abstraction chain of labor, power, and capital, which results in the bourgeois idiot type for whom any means are justified to emerge as the last man standing in the capitalist eschaton. Or as Marx puts it: "One capitalist always kills many." And given enough time, he will kill them all. This "only one and its own," to misquote Max Stirner, is the antipole to the clone or zombie, which only operate as many. But both poles imply active potentials of the same present-time apocalypse depicted in Us: the humanoids attempt to storm the rich man's bunker, but the struggle takes place in the financialized psyche of the individual.

*Two capitalisms?*—Wendy's world is full of happy idiots. And they are doubly happy: firstly as bourgeois idiots or unique *multi-singletons,* and secondly as generic idiots or *single Theys.* It's a world in which everyone realizes themselves without ever experiencing themselves; that is, abstract movements of capital and semiotic operators are turning us into real abstractions, including generic product schemes that unify behavior, thought, and appearance. At the same time standpoints are singularizing to the point of absurdity; that is, we can only understand or be understood from our idiosyncratic point of view, which can already be observed in current discursive practice: Critique of one's point of view is only possible under the premise that a specific set of beliefs and discourses is shared, but this specific set is unique. So I believe in x and accept a critique of x only if the other person is essentially *me,* and this *me* criticizing myself would conveniently affirm myself, no matter what the discourse. This harmless and ubiquitous "madness" of the self is not far from Stalin's famous letters on the necessity of self-criticism as the highest communist virtue—as defined by Stalin. Or take the fierce advocacy of free speech by the likes of Elon Musk, who regularly issues threats against company whistleblowers or online criticism of him. This isn't just a performative contradiction, it's the basis of communication. In other words, the whole discursive act is farcical because it's based on an *ultimate* self. In the world of multi-singletons critique is either impossible or meaningless. Everyone speaks an (according to Wittgenstein) impossible private language, has a private religion, owns private property, is absolutely unique, unintelligible, and incomparable, yet at the same time completely identical with one another as single Theys. Mutual understanding is based on coincidence, and yet everyone is indistinguishable from one another in this intimate coexistence. What Bernard Stiegler calls the "end of the future" emerges as a bifocal vision of the present. On the one hand we have a total differentiation from self-politics to the solipsist proprietor, on the other a total generalization of communication and forms of expression. Isolation leads to a multitude of stand-alones, yet at the same time idiosyncrasy is embedded in all market procedures, which come down to the total leveling of all. Almost everyone owns a cellphone (from the oil billionaire to the war refugee), and everyone uses the cellphone in their own way. But at the same time everyone uses it in the same way, defined by, say, standardized finger gestures. In Wendy's ad the simultaneity of idiosyncratizing monopolies—leading to maximum product differentiation—and polypoles ("perfect competition")—leading to complete homogenization, is dealt with in such a way that the individual people aren't portrayed as anonymous personalizations of the They in identical clone form, but as individual persons. However, depending on how close you look, they are all as unique as they are identical. In this sense we might also speak of the presence of two capitalisms in the one subject: a zoomed-out and a zoomed-in variety; one that dissolves structures, one that restructures. Félix Guattari points to these two forms with his model of the worldwide integrated capitalism that has been subliminally present since industrialization in the eighteenth century and has only come to maturity in the present: "These transformations do not imply that the new capitalism completely takes the place of the old one. There is rather coexistence, stratification, and hierarchalization of capitalisms at different levels." Guattari introduces two levels equivalent to my two trajectories:

a) Bourgeois idiotism, comprising "traditional segmentary capitalisms, terriorialized onto Nation-states, and deriving their unity from a monetary and financial mode of semiotization."

b) Planetary idiotism, that is, "a World-Wide Integrated Capitalism, that no longer rests on the sole mode of semiotization of financial and monetary Capital, but more fundamentally, on a whole set of technico-scientific, macrosocial and microsocial, and mass media procedures of subjection."

The one capitalism creates multi-singletons, the other single Theys. For it's also the inner logic of territorialized tribalism that once the identification machine has been started, more and more sub-identities are produced, which are then an expression of the claim to authentic territory and identity in time. *The process of individuation is suspended at both poles*, despite subjects at both poles claiming the opposite. Idiot types, whether "sheeple" or a multitude of egomaniacs, believe they act individually. A frenetic nationalist, although babbling the same about his homeland as all his compatriots, insists on his individuality, as does the sales manager who repeats ad slogans when privately justifying, say, her company's green philosophy. The two capitalisms represent the extremes of reified de-individualization: featureless users or supersubjects that *only* have features. In this line of thought the humanoids—from the superhero to the supermonster—aren't metaphors of inhumanness or superhumanness. They are the symbolic poles of the everyday struggle for the vanishing individual.

*Slick signifiers*—Idiocratic poles are often dealt with in sci-fi films. In SURROGATES (2009), for example, public life is populated by androids operated by their controllers at home, who are a dystopian version of the ancient *idiotes*. Surrogates are sent out into the world because their degenerate host organisms are no longer capable of doing so and have to interface with their public selves from within the techno-bubbles where they vegetate on private incomes. Here too we have two poles: the supposedly authentic, private world with social tensions (marital crisis, work stress, and so on), and the exaggeratedly hassle-free humanoids in the outside world, as planetary representatives of the single Theys. Human body and avatar are in a continual intimate relationship to one another without feeling one another, and yet, in an idiocratic sense, they are one and the same, merely representing two subject poles of the one planetary condition. What James Cameron's AVATAR (2009) plays through in a reactionary take on the exotic tribe takes place in SURROGATES in the surface tension of the everyday. The filmic iconodulism references real life, where homebodies physiologically emulate surrogates, that is, when users have plastic surgery in order to resemble their online alter egos (also known as "Snapchat dysmorphia"). The film brings the deformed body to light as part of the inherently contradictory production cycle that determines the relationship between our online and offline personas. Compared with THE TRUMAN SHOW (1998), where the protagonist escapes the manufactured illusion, in SURROGATES the revolutionary who agitates against the surrogate universe turns out to be a surrogate himself.

*Dynamic stasis*—Idiocratic projections penetrate all levels of the imagination. An abyss gapes on every corner, and one idiot pole immediately calls forth another one without there being any kind of synthesis. Nathan Brown describes this constellation as "dialectic at a standstill" and illustrates the absorption of difference and inclusion with a poem by Steve McCaffery, from the band *Shifters* (1976). It reads:

you
are what
i

am apart
from

what
i

is
a part

of

The beginning can be read as "you are what I am," or as "you are what I am apart from." Participation and separation become ontological functions; planetary idiocy and the singularity of the person are an aspect of the sentence. You are what I am, but at the same time this I identical with you is part of something that disregards you, that in complete isolation lacking all identity is paradoxically identical with all others. This dynamic stasis defines the current aporia of the idiocratic condition, in which all subjects become identical in their isolation. Hall of mirrors and windowless unit in one. The reach of the new idiot has merged with the planetary condition. The will of the clone is alienated (but permanently incorporated) and the appetitive will of the monads is unintelligible (but permanently conveyed). The *volonté générale* wants its opposite, exposing its will to absurdity.

*Misrecognition*—The utopia of the individual consists in it never being able to come true without questioning everyone's uniqueness. And liberal egalitarianism can never be fulfilled without happiness being found in the figure of the individual. We're always individual in relation to something overriding, sharable: a group, an organization, a commons. Politicians, for example, behave individually when they break away from party discipline. Citizens behave individually when they aren't civil, when they not only refuse given norms but turn them into something else and act innovatively. And vice versa: in his examination of the hippie culture of the 1960s, Pasolini referred to the de-individualizing tendencies of an individualist protest movement, a point echoed recently by Jonathan Touboul in his study "The Hipster Effect: When Anti-Conformists All Look the Same" (2019). After the paper appeared in the *MIT Technology Review*, a disgruntled young man called the editorial office threatening legal action to obtain the removal of a photograph in which he appeared, as it had been published without his permission. It showed a bearded young man in a woolen cap, and was intended to portray a "prototypical hipster." The young man considered his personality rights violated through his stigmatization as a hipster. It turned out, however, that the person in the photograph was in fact a professional model. The caller had mistaken someone portraying a typical hipster for himself, only to complain about being stigmatized as a typical hipster, thus brilliantly confirming Touboul's study, or as an editor put it: "Hipsters look so much alike that they can't even tell themselves apart from each other." This isn't just an amusing case of misidentification. It shows up a fundamental aspect of today's idiocratic condition: that we can't distinguish anymore between the private and the public image of ourselves, either because we are only ourselves, *multi-singletons,* or because we think and behave as all others, as *single Theys.* And this condition turns even the staunchest non-conformists into conformists.

*Division*—The main contradiction of today's liberal societies is that they are increasingly calibrated to the free development of personal identity, while the ultimate realization of this goal makes society and therefore every individual impossible. If this contradiction isn't synthesized in some way, we maneuver ourselves into an impossible society—an idiocracy. According to the German philosopher Christoph Menke, the contradiction reflects a divided subject: "The division of freedom is internal. On one side the free subject is something absolutely special, going even as far as the idiotic, the unfathomably unintelligible. The liberal order makes this into a subject that only follows its own interests. On the other side we want the generality, that is, the equality of all. [...] In this the liberal order has ascribed the two aspects of freedom to separate spheres, the economic and the governmental. And in the separation of these two aspects they lose their liberating and transcending force. Both sides become unfree in liberalism." This division is based on the incompatibility of the general and the particular, as discussed above. In our context, however, it isn't dependent on how liberal or authoritarian a political system is, it's just channeled differently—through the authoritarian figure of a "dear leader," say, as the Ubuesque figuration of the absurd. Recent surges in strongman attitude in political or economic leadership are only desperate attempts to fight the inherent idioticizing nature of capital and turn the process of individuation into a farce from the position of the last man standing. This is the reason why billionaire political surrogates like Peter Thiel believe in the monopoly as the real driver of the market—the economic equivalent of the only one—or as Thiel put it back in 2009: "The fate of our world may depend on the effort of a single person." Competition for Thiel is only the foreplay of the ultimate libidinal act of the last one—presumably him—with himself, which is why he doesn't believe "that freedom and democracy are compatible"—a point that resonates well with the conservative mainstream of today. The point is not to secure a competition but to secure a win. In the United States the practice of gerrymandering and voter suppression is analogous to Thiel's economic line of thinking, not to speak of Trump's chronic inability to accept defeat. The point being that if you consider yourself the last one there is no defeat, and if you have a monopoly on meaning there is no electorate—this "dictatorship of the self" is literally what idiocracy does to the mind. But it is a disappearing self; all that remains is an empty shell. If we abstract from the particularities of politics to the base level, what Adorno claims about subjectivity in late modernity is ubiquitous: "Individual self-preservation succeeds only as far as self-formation fails." Individuals attain their subject status through their ruin; the subject jumps into a hole, dragging the reason why into the depths, or gulping it down like a fast-food menu ...

## PHENOMENOLOGY OF THE MANY

*Capitalist trinity*—Wendy's world has a central attractor, its hole. Since all the runners' trajectories converge like the rods bound into the fasces, this world is structurally "fascist." But this is only one aspect, as the people don't march into the hole in uniformed rank and file, but "individually." Also the hole doesn't parallel the charismatic presence of a leader; on the contrary, it matches his absence. Wendy's image isn't that of the traditional fascist mass with a *Führer* to guide it into the abyss; rather, it is Guattari's image of planetary fascism. In order to grasp the whole of the political allegory, Wendy's image needs to be supplemented by two others like a triptych: one variant in which the hole is filled in, and all the individuals run senselessly across the plain; and one in which there are countless holes and countless Wendies all producing their own crispy hamburgers:

$$\circ\,\circ\,\circ\,\circ\,\circ\,\circ\,\circ\,\circ \rightarrow @$$

This triptych—depicting a kind of capitalist "trinity"—gives us the presence of the great hole attracting the many, an empty plateau without a hole, on which the many run around aimlessly, and a multitude of holes that surround the many (think of malls, where customers are torn between the variety of attractions). Subjects evolve in a simultaneity of "fascist" (running towards a central hole), "idiotic" (running towards no holes), and "bureaucratic" (running towards countless holes) relations. They don't just run toward one central attractor, as with a monopoly, but are also surrounded by numerous attractors or move aimlessly with no attractor, becoming attractors themselves, merging into the product scheme of self-referential semiotic operations, and so on.

Analogous to the Christian Trinity, which knows only the one belief in the one God, this capitalist trinity is based on a single mode of attraction: the general equivalent, or capital as the one semiotic operator of meaning. Here idiocracy can be understood as a multimodal field in the form of myriads of online users acting out the egalitarian potential of digital capitalism (any "idiot" can say, do, or become anything); and simultaneously as a dominant mode of attraction that sublates the individual interest in the alienated interest of all. Translated into current market logic we can imagine a future situation in which every human on earth has become an influencer, meets other influencers, all recommending each other identical products with nobody understanding the overall planetary situation. This recalls Kafka's parable of kings and messengers. Given the choice of becoming kings or the kings' messengers, "they all wanted to be messengers. That is why there are only messengers, racing through the world and, since there are no kings, calling out to each other the messages that have now become meaningless." This meaningless racing through the world, while constantly messaging or commenting about it—as most of us do daily—has become the central image of our capitalist totality. In this world the most absurd transaction will also be the most reasonable one.

*Stars*—If we dive further into the manifold of singularized society, we can imagine subjects modeled as point-like attractors, each equipped with their own "magnetic" potential. The most attractive among them—commonly known as "stars"—are not impacted by other attractions: stars typically don't wait but let you wait, provided you are not a star, and if you are it depends on who is the bigger star. Stars don't stand in line, and if they do they stand as if being waited for. Stars do what they want, and what they want is what they do. Stars sometimes do adapt to the behavior of the common fan, in the way a popstar creates, meets, or imitates the taste of his or her followers, acting as one of them, not behaving like a celebrity is expected to. Every star—from the lowest level of starification, like a local star, to the superstar—is self-contained and autonomous, totally distinct and thus featureless.

All stars have the same aura that says: "I accomplished something extraordinary." Since in principle "everybody can become a star," wannabe stars act as stars before being known as stars, which is what makes many participants in TV talent shows act like idiots (which reminds me of how the Austrian satirist Karl Kraus once joked that he was world famous, only nobody knew about it). If a favorable market dynamic does in fact make one of the many would-be stars into a superstar, a swarm forms around him or her and follows its star at every turn—to great effect: social media accounts feature popstars, footballers, politicians, actors, and other celebs, each with hundreds of millions of followers. The star can post something online—even a single word—and the followers lap it up in their millions and participate in the resulting meme dynamics. Despite this semiotic reliability, the myriads of followers can't be directly exploited politically because everyone is a potential star in their own right. Everyone, wanting to be a star, eagerly collects followers, improving their magnetism and market reach as influencers. This "individualism" saves the many from collective madness caused by singularization. But revised downwards, stars are only stars in their niches and unknown in their neighboring worlds—which becomes obvious every time you are confronted with the name of a social-media star you never heard of with about half a billion followers.

*Social magnetism*—In the idiocratic coordinate system every subject oscillates between a single They, a featureless mass point, or a point of potential starification. Stars are attractors (@) and single Theys (o) run around aimlessly until they become followers. There are three possible ways to interact:

$$@ \rightarrow @$$
$$@ \rightarrow o$$
$$o \rightarrow o$$

Either two stars meet (@ → @), who then respect or ignore one another. Cooperation between stars is difficult, impossible, or disastrous—

think of star-packed films that bomb at the box office—because stars only function within their own niche world. There's no space imaginable in which stars would be inclined to form a union, say, or march in the street as a collective of stars to protest against something. Rather, they are inclined to widen their own star space and create the conditions of new star formation ("a star is born"). Or a star meets a single They (@ → o), who becomes a fan. The fan can stick with @ or move on to a different @. @ can also be a person, an "automatic subject," an institution, generally an attraction. Finally there is the possibility of a meeting between single Theys (o → o). Like the stars above they may have little use for one another because they may be looking for an @. But if they each become aware of their own magnetism, a servant–servant dialectic arises and releases them from existing attractions; or, to apply a space metaphor, it is as if they were using gravitational pull to get into a different orbit or to leave the solar aka star system altogether. This metaphor approximates to the class-overturning proletariat, in as much as the endeavor brings about a social pole that generates an attraction different from the existing one, or basically reinvents the social magnetism of star and follower. Otherwise the dialectic of the many, as in Wendy's world, would just produce more of the same stars instead of getting rid of starification. Simply founding a new company changes nothing. And if you only want change, you end up founding a company ...

*Phenomenological fracture*—The operative structures of Wendy's world imply abstract power relations that, once concrete, can turn the unpolitical many into a political multitude. If you're waiting in line, it means you have some business (paying something, applying for something, leaving the country); it means that the others in line have the same status as you; and it means that you don't have the power to complete your business on your own terms. Rather, you have to wait for someone else to decide. In a "topological" sense you become a featureless, one-dimensional point-subject, as far as you are subject to this structure— as one applicant among many, at the mercy of the authorities, or as a refugee in a detention center or as a single lifeless point floating in the Mediterranean:

•

At this *point of ultimate humiliation* what Achille Mbembe calls the "becoming black of the world" comes into play, that is, humanity's subjection to the principle of general enslavement and at the same time the vision and subjectivation of its liberation, the birth of a universal perspective from the death of the subaltern: "The question of the world [...] has been within us since a human being of bone, flesh, and spirit made its first appearance under the sign of the Black Man, as *human-merchandise, human-metal*, and *human-money*." This question of the world gives rise to "the project of a world that is coming, [...] whose destination is universal" (ibid.). From this perspective the subject points of the world (o) shouldn't be seen as accumulations of colorless individuals but as the zero expression of the universal individual, who takes on "color"—in both its historical and visionary sense.

*The universalization of the opposite*—This phenomenology of the many leads us to a reconsideration of Don DeLillo's assertion that the future belongs to crowds. Rather, its ownership is shared by the multitude of singletons and the "singletude" of Theys. Taking Stiegler's "end of the future" into account we could say that our current state comes down to Philip Bobbitt's hypothesis of the continuum of the market state—the infinite extension of capitalism through time—as symbolized in three symbolic scenarios: meadow, park, and garden. In the meadow every protagonist can do his business unheeded, and liberal arbitrariness dominates: "In this world, success comes to those who nimbly exploit the fast-moving, evanescent opportunities brought about by high technology and the global marketplace" (Bobbitt). Protagonists are guardians in the park, where there are bureaucratic mechanisms of state control—the condition of the park "reflects a society in which the values and attitudes of the managerial market-state have prevailed" (ibid.).

And in the garden each protagonist is the unrestricted ruler of his or her territory. Control is a part of cultivation; state and identity coincide; that is, states in this scenario "have become more and more ethnocentric, and more and more protective of their respective cultures" (ibid.). In a nutshell: "In a meadow all is profusion, randomness, variety. A park is for the most part publicly maintained, highly regulated with different sectors for different uses. A garden is smaller, more inwardly turned—it aims for the sublime, not the efficient or the just" (ibid.). In this type of triptych agents of change wander around the meadows, parks, and gardens—as entities in between—and civilizing progress is accompanied by all kinds of technological, cultural, and political regression, which fragments the crowds and turns the many against one another. Many historical revolts immediately suffocate and yield to the "parable of the revolution" (Egon Friedell), which ends in a state of affairs identical with what came before, or worse, as in Egypt following the Arab Spring, where the anti-authoritarian revolution has become another lost hope. What's worse than finding out that the future has already happened, that nothing better can be expected? When history turns out to be a repeating farce, then Beckett's encouragement to "fail better" no longer applies—rather, sometimes one hopes that self-righteous political projects "better fail." Perhaps we've already reached this point, for the usual leftwing calculations regarding the emancipation of the many no longer seem to add up. State socialism has entirely merged with state capitalism and "globalist" logic. If you want to make sure you can produce for a pittance and exploit the workforce to the maximum, invest in commu-capitalist China. If you still think you can masquerade as socialism with a party nomenklatura, engage in organized cynicism like the Venezuelan Chavists. Moreover, the various New Deals that flared in populist leftwing political campaigns (Sanders, Corbyn, Syriza, Podemos, and so on) failed to gain traction, while the systemic regulating screws of capitalism no longer appear to allow a return to the old social democracy. Even Roosevelt's New Deal was a compromise negotiated with the industrial magnates in order to avert a proletarian revolt after the Great Depression (the magnates would also have come to an agreement with the equally short-lived swell of America-first fascism). For today's swarm of idiocrats social democracy is too reflective, too undynamic, too Scandinavian (except when there is a war or a pandemic, then checks are sent out to the populace). For this reason the current New Deal was given a "green" suffix to bolster the belief in capitalism. But grassroots initiatives, which emphasize the self-organization and networking of leftwing groupings, also lack realistic market trajectories, perhaps because they have no shared social vision and the acephalous Leviathan crushes all young shoots. The Occupy tents have disappeared, but the banks have swollen along with the fortunes of the fortune 100; the richest man on earth has a net worth of well over 200 billion dollars. The result is a new symbiosis, as some of today's grassroots and climate activists are funded by the green-energy sector or by whichever billionaire comes along. Which of the many and which of the ones does which future belong to? Not the crowds, not the multitude, not the political movements, not the sponsored niches. Franco Berardi therefore calls for a general liberation from the claws of "economic semiotization," the flight from the general scheme of politics: "Only by dissociation (not by contradiction) can different forms emerge." For this he envisages a "poetical potency of estrangement." In other words, back to the old idiot by means of the new idiot; then something might happen with the opposite. But beyond this hope, the ways of the global situation are becoming more and more mysterious. How can we give our ignorance a new meaning? How can we *not* pretend to know better?

*Perspectivism*—The switch from Nietzsche's aesthetic agency to Kierkegaard's ethical agency to Marx's political agency doesn't invalidate the aesthetic or the ethical, but emphasizes the interplay of action and expression on the level of the many: the ethicization of aesthetics in activism, the politization of aesthetics in state socialism, the aestheticization of ethics in post-Fordism, the aestheticization of aesthetics in post-fascism. In classical Fordist organization, programmers, corporations, or state apparatuses established material attractors and, through interpellation mechanisms, endowed the many with features such as a work ethic, a culture, an identity. This occurred within strict boundaries between working hours and living hours, workplace and dwelling, and regulated public life. The theory of proletarianization begins within this geometrical order, which appears from this perspective to be levered out by global migration, for example, as it questions familiar mechanisms. Migration, as has become evident during the past decade, appears to be the vehicle of a new proletariat that sets the geopolitical tectonics in motion and asks questions about an (inter)nationalization of the labor movement that Marx had addressed in relation to Irish labor migration, for example. Whatever answers are given, there is a dominant promise of emancipatory salvation. This directs Negri & Hardt in their theorization of the multitude, which they see as levering out the order of production methods. But the idiocratic condition is more "advanced," radical, paradoxical, complex. It describes, for example, "a boundary-less form that ignores older distinctions between market and society, market and world, or market and person" (Zuboff). In this line of thought, migration as social structuring is ubiquitous. We migrate as soon as we step outside. Work has filtered everywhere, has infiltrated the living hours of the many, who no longer isolate themselves from its attractors but take them home with them. This complex derives from the interweaving of intellectual and manual labor, of complex and simple work, which goes along with the deconstruction of political representation—"You don't represent us!" was the paradigmatic call of the Indignados who assembled on the Puerta del Sol in Madrid in May 2011. Just as the occupational area breaks up our leisure time, the political will is unravelling and is no longer attached to a party, organization, or movement, not even to a standpoint, as reflected in the above-discussed idiotypical figurations: the will to absurdity, dialectic of incompetence, freneticism, the only one and its own, planetary idiocy, and so on. This is regressive in that the collapse of representation hints at a final condition that is undermining civilization as such (comparable to the heat death of the universe). And it is emancipatory in that with the collapse of representation new horizons are continually being evoked (comparable to a supernova that brings about new stars). In the words of Paolo Virno, the significance of non-representative democracy "is in no way interstitial, marginal or residual," but lies in its "concrete appropriation and re-articulation of the knowledge/power unity." Idiots—here in the sense of weird agitators—set the congealed forms in motion through their deployment of the absurd. It would be like Wendy building a tower where everybody expected a hole. The same motion is the basis of an emancipated public. The idiocratic multitude is no representative collective, the new proletariat no *Volk*, no casteless caste, but an expression of the "general intellect" (Marx), of a human potential—a Cartesian zero point. As general intellect, the emancipated many are a pre-reflective category of organization, similarly to the way in which the unreflecting self corresponds to the real—in Rosa Luxemburg's sense of political organizing, they are spontaneous. Here we can see the potential and the danger emanating from socio-physics and computational economics as tools for rational planning. They can be welcomed, on the one hand, as in the long run the organization of the many shouldn't be subject to irrational market laws whose increasingly complex formalization in economic formulae deceives us with an apparent rationality. On the other hand (which is to be imagined as the same "hand" as above), since universal reason isn't constituted in the formalization of wisdom, but by the critique of its form, it is precisely in the rational endeavor to establish global control over complex systems that the irrationality of market and power is reproduced. Big data is a "humanizing force" (Alex Pentland) until it isn't, turning reason into totalitarian rationalism. Idiocracy stands for both the difficulty and the necessity of defining the emancipatory realm of the many as a realm of absurdity and contradiction, of political multimodality. This necessity also fosters a *parafactual* ability that world-optimizers, touts, and tech gurus seem to lack: the flexibility to deal with different sets of symbols in a surprising, even naive way. Beyond everything possible and expected. The motto being: if I have to be an idiot, I'll be a complete one.

# IDIOPRACTICE

*Onto the pedestal ... and be an idiot.*
Erwin Wurm

*Zeroed future*—Asked if he was optimistic or pessimistic, Pasolini replied: "I am an apocalyptic." The eschatological perspective is an idiocratic driver. The end is everywhere, it already prevails in Max Stirner's
"owner," the radical foreshortening of social idiocy, the idea of being the
only survivor at the end of days. However, from an idiocratic perspective, the end of days is always now, and the apocalypse has to do with
the meaning gained from this present end: What comes after the goal?
How do you live after the happy end? What comes after happiness? And
what comes after that? For as Don DeLillo writes in *Cosmopolis*: "The
future becomes insistent." Such considerations lead to a practice that
Antonio Negri once called "humanism after the death of man." Bernard
Stiegler similarly discerns the rise of the Neganthropocene, an organo-
logical response to the social death of information. These transanthro-
pological and neohumanist perspectives share an openness to the end,
and thus imply a practice of new beginnings, a permanent or evolving
future, if you will, that counters the ending of things. This originally
avant-garde perspective echoes today, for example, in Achille Mbembe's hope for a "collective resurgence of humanity," which is recurrently
refracted in the prism of idiocractic reason, for it applies to the many
ones who remain only the reflection of the new that blinds them. Methods of production bleed into one another; genres are so porous that it's
impossible to keep them within bounds; there is no collective human
direction; movement is confounded by the babble of power and opinion. Some protagonists count on their messages outlasting the inflation

of signs: "The poet has the final word. Not now. Not in the meantime, as long as everyone is noisily and separately talking to themselves. But later, when the voices subside and the earth's all ears" (Botho Strauß). The "final word" is the literary hope of the only one. But in this final present, will thing and non-thing, human and non-human, poetry and interpretation merge, until even the end as criterium and the final word as word become unrecognizable? Until everything is in place and nothing disappears any more? "What we excrete comes back to consume us," writes DeLillo. But on the other hand isn't it the task of the critical imagination to continue questioning the logic and contradiction of the end, to dissolve or join ends, to take up loose ends or link them to other ends? "'Any road.' said Carlyle, 'this simple Entenpfuhl road, will lead you to the end of the World.' But the Entepfuhl road, if it is followed all the way to the end, returns to Entepfuhl; so that Entepfuhl, where we already were, is the same end of the world we set out to find" (Pessoa). So to the very end—and in a certain sense returning to the beginning—we look to the practical options that result from this endgame.

*Refuge*—The traditional philosophical advice for the good life is generally anti-apocalyptic. The idea being that if everyone behaves, all will be well and the ending will be a happy one. Since Plato's *Apology of Socrates* this philosophical attitude has been content to recommend contemplative retreat in the face of the incalculability of the many. A life without self-examination, says Socrates, isn't worth living. Put differently: unexamined life intrinsically has no ending. At the same time experience shows that this cozy "recourse to the subject" (Adorno) proves inadequate in public life. In order to avoid citizen-solipsism, we shouldn't lose sight of the broader picture. We should always relate the particular, which we meet at home, to the general of the *agora*. The political axiom is: *Get down to essentials!* Operate on the small scale but think big and work towards an opportunity to take the floor. As Pessoa writes, this is also a practice of sensibility: "True experience comes from restricting our contact with reality while increasing our analysis of that contact. In this way our sensibility becomes broader and deeper, because everything is in us." A different kind of philosophical advice is more impatient and more outwardly insistent. It leads us via Kant's Enlightenment ethics to Habermas's primate of "communicative reason," that is, to the public and universal call: *Be reasonable!* Stop being idiots. Sit round a table and negotiate the future together. But in the course of reflexive modernization, in which every maxim "is becoming its own theme" (Beck), this call for maximum cooperation comes with dialectic rigor and a caveat. The call now is: *Be reasonably irrational!* Which encompasses the entire range of possibilities, including the reclusive sage.

*Inherent escapism*—Idiopractice, in the narrower sense *a performing of non-exploitable originality,* refers not so much to the move into the private or public arenas but to the escape from both home and marketplace. It refers to the overcoming of individual and collective positions and the creation of idiosyncratic spaces that resist control in a "simultaneity of a 'we' and an 'apartness'" (Wolfgang Müller), as called for by the 1980s Berlin avant-garde group Geniale Dilletanten ("inspired amateurs"). This corresponds to a political philosophy of the idiot that has stumbled through the first realm to arrive at the second in a constant search for a creative exit, which the Belgian-French "psychedelic" poet Henri Michaux once envisioned as follows: "I should like a multiple exit, shaped like a fan. An exit that never ends, an ideal exit, an exit such that having gone out I should immediately start to go out again." Idiopractice is seeking ways out that avoid the known routes. This approach seems as necessary as the philosophical retreat, for both public and private are compromised: media technology has made the home sinister; the round table has proved to be a trap, the public arena a chimaera, the equality of participants spurious; and on top of all that the discussion is eavesdropped by the same authority that enabled universal discourse. So the guiding principle of the functional idiot in evading usefulness is to cut and run, to disappear from the screen. Depending on the approach, this takes the form of techno-asceticism, strategic isolation, artistic orphanhood, the self-freak, total anonymization, anarchic runaway collectives, covering one's digital tracks, carving out niches.

In short, the desertion of compulsory contexts while avoiding the contaminated private or public arena. What does CIA analyst Joe Turner (Robert Redford) do in THREE DAYS OF THE CONDOR (1975) when he realizes that he can neither go home nor be seen in public? He attaches himself to an arbitrarily chosen person. He thus breaks a pattern and so becomes "invisible" to power. In today's political sphere clandestine groupings put up similar resistance by creating contingent systems or operating *erratically*, which is essentially how common idiots operate too. Breakaway figures start small revolts, much as Martin Page's idiot Antoine claims autonomy for himself. They don't always need to be individual protagonists either, but collective subjects like Luther Blissett, a pseudonym under which a number of political or artistic activists have been organizing protests or publishing work for decades. The Dadaist installation of the idiot is neither a singular nor a completed process. The aim of semiotic dropouts or "refugees" is the categorical refusal of instrumental reason and its custodians. This idiopractice of the many is our future too. It is more demonstrative and more definite than the intimate self-questioning path of the philosopher or than public involvement. It is also more disorganized and isolated, and not always "activist." This is shown by the case of an American who used the Trump election in 2016 as an opportunity to remove himself from the news loop for a year, sometimes walking around with sunglasses and earplugs. The *New York Times* dubbed him the "most selfish man in America" for this destructive act of evading his civic responsibility. But that's also the point: "civic responsibility" shouldn't automatically be understood as the solution for everything, but also as part of the problem. Here we have to read Martin's maxim in Voltaire's *Candide* bifocally: "'Let us set to work and stop proving things,' said Martin, 'for that is the only way to make life bearable.'" This is both a call to conformism (working without giving it a thought) and an escape from the claws of instrumental reason (not giving a thought to work), that is, it's an activity that can add to your vexation. For economic calculation comes into play as soon as you "give something a thought" these days—capital proposes, man disposes. The detour of instrumental reason therefore embraces not only the specialist discipline of political activism but also oddities such as the dying pensioner who, having stopped "proving things" a few years ago, wished to be buried with his favorite porno. This caused him trouble with the authorities and led to a public dispute about whether you can compel someone to take his death seriously. The pensioner had evaded the civic responsibility of a civilized demise.

*Micro-revolutions*—The creation of new types of vexation—and that means new political postulations that draw on the vocabulary of the old annoyances—is indebted to a situationist ethic that has been a feature of artistic activism since the 1950s. I refer not only to the Situationist International or the Lettrist International as specific historically relevant collectives, but primarily to the idiophile motif at work in them and noticeable in many groupings from recent decades, such as variants of Internet art, neoisms, parody religions (Discordianism), underground movements (No Wave Cinema), participatory networks (Association of Autonomous Astronauts) or globally operating artist groups (Adbusters, ®™ark, Yes Men, Superflex), guerillas of various kinds (Guerilla Girls, Spaßguerilla, Internationale Pâtissière), solo idiopractitioners (Monopoly Man), salons on idiocy as resistance, and so on. Whatever form these activities take, there is always creative entrepreneurship and some foundational act involved. Every vision of a commons is, as Achille Mbembe writes, "inseparable from the reinvention of community." All these idiophile founding mothers and fathers have their descendants, as shown by the Danish theater group Solvognen, who—disguised as Santa Clauses—distributed the articles on the shelves of a department store to its customers in 1974. This action later produced the ritualist movements of Santarchy or Santa Con in the United States. Socio-political idiopractice leads to both the ritualization of the individual case and to the idiosyncratization of conventions. It doesn't accept the political as a constant but "invents" it along with its actions. This even applies to the man who disguised himself as a polar bear and terrorized customers camping at four in the morning in front of a Midwest store before the Black Friday sale. After his arrest he declared that the action had been spontaneous and without ulterior motives, and that he'd do it again any time. But the political implication of this apolitics is immediately clear: the authorities will remove the dwellings of homeless people from the forecourts of shopping centers, but they will protect anyone spending the night there as a prospective consumer. Here the idiot takes on the role of a *parallel police* and draws attention to the absurdity of the status quo without offering a critique of capitalism (because it isn't necessary). As Monika Rinck concludes, "the idiot wishes to replace the general tension, understood and thus denied as mere functioning, with hypertension."

*Specialism-activism*—"Does the best of subversions not consist in disfiguring codes, not in destroying them?" Roland Barthes once asked. Idiopractice doesn't reflect on conditions but mutates along with them. The departmentalization of knowledge and power, the inflation of specialists, is paralleled by an idiopractice that intervenes in niche problems without wanting to save the entire world, so as to save the entire world. These idiopractitioners see the greater good in fragmented action, and they don't require legitimation for it. Typical are actions such as those of the Bristol grammar vigilante who made it his task to correct public spelling mistakes by nocturnally tampering with signs and shop logos with orthographical errors. But despite his appearance as a lone wolf, globally he is one of many. Under the name of Acción Ortográfica Quito, Ecuadorean idealists have been correcting public inscriptions for years, inspiring imitators around the world. These street editors are neither political activists nor artists. They should be understood more as idiosyncratic "officials" pursuing a personalization of the public services, comparable with street-cleaning or garbage disposal (remember the publicly engaged autistic "activist" A. I described in part one). The important thing is to distinguish the activities of these lone operators from community organizers or political activists, for these are motivated by political, aesthetic, or private interests, while the idiopractitioners to a certain extent work disinterestedly, at the level of the crudest pattern. Since they work from the standpoint of a totality, their subject, no matter how niche or idiosyncratic, is a total-ity. They gain no reward and remain anonymous, that is, they adopt the form of *some idiot* who gets up to something. Seen from his confident zero position, complaints about vandalized signs leave the grammatical avenger from Bristol cold. "It's more of a crime to have the apostrophes wrong," he asserts. If you take the multitude seriously, you also have to pay political tribute to the "agitpop" of isolated ne'er-do-wells. Pessoa speaks for them: "We possess nothing, for we don't even possess our-selves. We have nothing because we are nothing." What matters politi-cally, says Ernesto Laclau, isn't generic variety but a variety of contra-diction: "A globalized capitalism creates myriad points of rupture and antagonisms [...] and only an overdetermination of this antagonistic plurality can create global anti-capitalist subjects capable of carrying out a struggle worth the name. And, as all historical experience shows, it is impossible to determine a priori who the hegemonic actors in this struggle will be. [...] All we know is that they will be the outsiders of the system, the underdogs [...] the heterogeneous." In the end, inspired by the will to absurdity, *everybody* will be an outsider.

*Idiostrategies*—Idiopractice includes confrontative, productive, casual-ist, or everyday idiostrategies: product sabotage, overidentifying into normcore, alienating public communication, exposing corrupt individ-uals, institutions, and corporations, autonomizing one's own spaces, hedonistically refusing to work, or anonymizing practices in order to sidestep discredited political positions. From an idiocratic point of view both subversion and convention are "activist." Just as the semi-otic operator of capitalism extends around the globe, potentially any act can add to the canvas of aesthetics and politics. Dostoyevsky's Myshkin is socially "effective" solely in being a thoroughly good per-son, that is, an idiot. More simply conceived, even the most inconspicu-ous gestures can provoke or annoy if they go against the usual injunc-tions—whether this means standing still when others are on the move, laughing out loud when others hold theirs in check, appearing when no one else does, senseless rituals ... "Take your pants off before you fight," said Yoko Ono. The Dadaistic enjoyment of "active simplicity" is a stigma and therefore also an opportunity, as can be seen in the various forms of craftivism, in which "domestic" activities are deployed to political ends. The many possibilities of idiopractice show that political and aesthetic agitation don't need to be invented, for the idiot and idiotic activity have always been around as ur-usurpers. They slumber as zeroed expression or derp face even in the serious grimaces of this world. Grand strategists turn out to be the biggest fools, and sophisticated entrepreneurs morph into tweeters. The idiotic mode is always upending, creating disturbances, errors, crashes, innovations, blindness, sightings—the question, then, is whether, where, and when we should "dare more idiocy" or not—and it can be derived not just from a practice that creates saboteurs, jokers, singularities, or pathological cases. It may be so that "if the freedom isn't in me, then I won't have it no matter where I go" (Pessoa), but this "no matter where" is the precondition of every freedom, the precondition of a *prefigurative politics*. Such a politics settles onto the new conditions and roots around in them, like Ubu, at the same time: "The new political art (if it is possible at all) will have to hold [...] to its fundamental object – the world space of multinational capital – at the same time at which it achieves a breakthrough to some as yet unimaginable new mode of representing this last, in which we may again begin to grasp our positioning as individual and collective subjects" (Fredric Jameson). Today's idiocratic energy is aimed against the representation of this "world space." One day it will have to embed Ubu's chaosmic drag marks in a future museum of decerebration—possibly as a "hotchpotch of banalities, prejudices, stereotypes, absurd situations – a whole free association of everyday life" (Guattari).

*Bifocality*—"Don't I have an ass like everyone else?" asks Ubu. In a wider sense idiopractice doesn't just stand for a confusion or correction of signs, a general regression, or the willed death of image and language, again, "full of sound and fury, signifying nothing," as befits the old idiot, but for something much more radical, namely what Guattari, writing about "chaosmic immanence" calls a "dance of chaos and complexity." There are many ways of seeing this modus operandi of (anti) social life. I have called it idiocracy—the rule of the own, with all the complexities and impossibilities it entails. But *koinocracy*, the rule of the shared can never really be separated from idiocracy. Idiopractice creates new sensoria and new ways of seeing from the creative side of the new idiot. But blindness also reproduces itself many times over in a world that sees more and more. We don't know where social blueprints are worked out, or what kind; we don't know what content is kept on which servers; we don't know which utopias the arts are channeling; we don't know which deeds have which consequences. But our ignorance is new every time, and brings new questions and new ways of seeing with it. In the post-avant-garde age everyone sleeps in the lap of capital and everyone is in the vanguard. It's impossible to make for one side without considering the other. We need to follow the path that Jameson calls "dialectic imperative": "Marx powerfully urges us to do the impossible, namely, to think this development positively and negatively all at once; to achieve, in other words, a type of thinking that would be capable of grasping the demonstrably baleful features of capitalism along with its extraordinary and liberating dynamism simultaneously within a single thought, and without attenuating any of the force of either judgment. We are somehow to lift our minds to a point at which it is possible to understand that capitalism is at one and the same time the best thing that has ever happened to the human race, and the worst." You have to wish, as Friedrich Engels puts it, "that the capitalist economy should develop at a truly spanking pace." Your conviction is part of the destruction. But what is the significance of an activity that bows to events in the same way that it refuses them? Why should you do something and not nothing? Bifocality means recognizing, with recourse to a Dadaist precept, that thought and action take place this side of incoherency, therefore that a strategy is as incoherent as a non-strategy. If you think you can overcome capitalism, you are an idiot—but on two counts: an idiot who wants the impossible, and an idiot because only an idiot can realize the impossible.

*Alarm*—The undermining of the status quo is a mechanism inherent in the status quo. If, as Althusser notes, ideology is always "already there," its negation aka utopia is even more readily "there." The way out of this predetermined fate is ubiquitously signposted in cultural production, though one needs some idiopractical "reason" to understand the subliminal messaging inherent in the popular mainstream. The "revolutionary leaders" of the Marvel universe, for example, continuously teach us that it's no longer a question of optimizing capitalism but of surviving it. The cinematic superheroes hurl their collective message into the heart of industrialized prosperity. All that superpower posturing and goodwill community-building, as in the AVENGERS series, showcases a global consciousness driven by the future societal collapse, which is addressed each time the universe is "threatened" by something or someone. Since a universe cannot be threatened, having no outside, the real message here is that the whole is a threat emerging from itself. The whole—or the hole in Wendy's world—is addressed in every appearance of a supervillain, as if it was using the film apocalypse to talk to human kind: "The end is nigh," says Thanos, the most powerful of the powerful. Yet, to reference Kafka's parable, Thanos is not a king but a messenger.

*The rest*—Idiopractice ultimately means than I can only find a way out of my "self-imposed immaturity" (Kant) if I don't completely understand myself, if I remain a beginner in relation to my feelings, my knowledge, my impulses, if I accept a new myth of the self. Deleuze writes: "What one says comes from the depths of one's ignorance, the depths of one's own underdevelopment." Where the will to absurdity becomes apparent as an option, idiopractice becomes recognizable and indeed serviceable. A similar thing applies to the modulations of ur-amateurism: Alfred Jarry's figure, in his want of know-how, generates new absurd know-hows from decerebration to pataphysics. However, today's real-world Ubus are still imperfect idiopractitioners of power. Actors have become presidents and presidents actors, comedians have founded parties and entered the EU parliament, and in 1967 a foot powder was elected mayor of an Ecuadorean town—but the intersectional field of what matters and what doesn't is much wider. It's conceivable for a meme to become president one day. Is this good or is this bad? Depends on how good a meme it is. There seems to be at least a pataphysical indication that the real is digesting the real. This uroboric condition arises from the creative energy of idiocracy, which both challenges and calls for the "acephelous supranational world order" of empire. Currently thriving object-oriented ontologies provide only a more serious label for a farcical general tendency. Even the apolitical "brainless" Internet trend of planking was proof you could opt out anywhere—from operating theater to mountain peak—and that everyone was up for any triviality anytime. Reification of consciousness is manifested in an individual reifying gesture. And perhaps it's only possible to set things in motion today as a motionless object. Here crypto-consciousness, there barter economy? Here *Gilet jaunes*, there breakdown triangles? Here activism, there stumbling blocks? "We have to think doing (*le faire*) even as it slides away, or even disconnects, from the project, the intention, and the question themselves," writes Jean-Luc Nancy in *What is To Be Done?* (2014). For "sense is never adequate to an object, a project, or an effect." What is needed here is Paolo Virno's analogy of virtuosity and politics in a centrifugal movement "from the One to the Many." The paradox of the herd calls for a paradoxical politics, and the road doesn't always follow the neatly marked route of the experts of fashionable discourse. An activity isn't an alibi for vapid reasoning, but even in Kant a reason of "pure spontaneity" and, thinking ahead, an incentive to active overextension: "Only the gift without hope of profit [...] can bring the present world out of the impasse," writes Bataille, insisting that "our sovereign moments, when nothing matters except what is there, what is sensible and captivating in the present are antithetical to the attention to the future and to the calculations without which there would be no labor." Virtuosity, spontaneity, and sovereignty transform into a kind of economy of festivity. Might this be conceivable as a new idiopractice? If everyone suddenly did the same thing, everything would be different.

## ACKNOWLEDGEMENTS

This book is a shorter and revised edition of the German original, published by diaphanes in 2019. My deepest gratitude goes to my publisher Michael Heitz for his support and his belief in this book, to Hendrik Rohlf for editing work, and to Michael Turnbull for his translation, which was funded by the Deutscher Übersetzerfonds through the NEUSTART KULTUR program of the Federal Government Commissioner for Culture and Media.

# LITERATURE

Adorno, Theodor W. *Aesthetic Theory*. Ed. Gretel Adorno and Rolf Tiedemann. Trans. Robert Hullot-Kentor. London, New York, 2004.

— "Erziehung nach Auschwitz." In *Erziehung zur Mündigkeit*. Frankfurt, 1971.

— *Minima Moralia: Reflections on a Damaged Life*. Trans. E. F. N. Jephcott (1974). London, New York, 2005.

— *Negative Dialectics*. Trans. E.B. Ashton. London, New York, 1973.

— "Postscriptum." In *Gesammelte Schriften*. Vol. 8, *Soziologische Schriften I*. Frankfurt, 2003.

— "Zum Verhältnis von Soziologie und Psychologie." In *Gesammelte Schriften*. Vol. 8. *Soziologische Schriften I*. Frankfurt, 2003.

Akerlof, George A. & Robert J. Shiller. *Phishing for Phools. The Economics of Manipulation and Deception*. Princeton, 2015.

Anders, Günther. *Die Antiquiertheit des Menschen*. Munich, 1961.

Arendt, Hannah. *The Human Condition* (1958). Chicago, 1998.

— *The Life of the Mind* (1971). New York, 1978.

Asimov, Isaac. *Wenn die Sterne verlöschen*. Rastatt, 1975.

Askin, N. & M. Mauskapf. "What Makes Popular Culture Popular? Product Features and Optimal Differentiation in Music." In *American Sociological Review SAGE*, September 6, 2017. https://doi.org/10.1177/0003122417728662

Azzouni, Safia & Uwe Wirth, eds. *Dilettantismus als Beruf*. Berlin, 2009.

Badiou, Alain. *Paulus – Die Begründung des Universalismus*. Zurich, Berlin, 2002.

Barthes, Roland. *Das Neutrum. Vorlesung am Collège de France 1977–1978*. Frankfurt, 2005.

— *Sade, Fourier, Loyola*. Trans. Richard Millar. Berkeley, 1989.

Barloewen, Constantin von. *Clown. Zur Phänomenologie des Stolperns*. Frankfurt, 1984.

Bartleby, "Are you stuck in a 'bullshit job'?" In *The Economist*, May 31, 2018. https://www.economist.com/business/2018/05/31/are-you-stuck-in-a-bullshit-job

Bataille, Georges. *Choix de lettres 1917–1962*. Paris, 1998. Quoted from Onofrio Romano, *Towards a Society of Degrowth*. New York, 2020.

— *The Accursed Share. An Essay on General Economy*. Vols. II and III. New York, 1991.

— et al. *The Sacred Conspiracy. The Internal Papers of the Secret Society of Acéphale and Lectures to the College of Sociology*. London, 2017.

Bauman, Zygmunt. *Culture as Praxis*. London, New Delhi, 1999.

— *Flaneure, Spieler und Touristen. Essays zu postmodernen Lebensformen*. Hamburg, 1997.

— *Flüchtige Zeiten: Leben in der Ungewissheit*. Hamburg, 2008.

— *Individualized Society*. Cambridge, 2001.

— *Liquid Modernity*, Cambridge, 2000.

— *Modernity and Ambivalence*. Cambridge, 1993.

— "Social media are a trap." Interview in *El Pais*, January 25, 2016. https://elpais.com/elpais/2016/01/19/inenglish/1453208692_424660.html

— "Zygmunt Bauman on the potential for political change." Interview in *e-flux conversations*, July 2016. https://conversations.e-flux.com/t/zygmunt-bauman-on-the-potential-for-political-change/4083

— & Carlo Bordoni. *State of Crisis*. Cambridge, 2014.

Bayer, Konrad. *idiot*. In *Sämtliche Werke*. Ed. Gerhard Rühm. Vienna, 1985.

Bazin, André. *Orson Welles. A Critical View*. Los Angeles, 1991.

Beck, Ulrich, *Risk Society. Towards a New Modernity*. Trans. Mark Ritter. London, 1992.

— & Anthony Giddens, Scott Lash. *Reflexive Modernization*. Stanford, 1994.

Beech, Amanda. "Begriff ohne Differenz. Das Problem des Generischen." In Avanessian, Armen et al., eds. *Realismus | Materialismus | Kunst*. Berlin, 2015.

Benjamin, Walter. *The Work of Art in the Age of Its Technological Reproducibility and Other Writings on Media*. Trans. Edmund Jephcott et al. Cambridge, London, 2008.

Benn, Gottfried. *Gesammelte Werke in vier Bänden*. Stuttgart, 1993.

Berardi, Franco. *Futurability. The Age of Impotence and the Horizon of Possibility*. New York, 2017.

Bertrand, Natasha. "Russia organized 2 sides of a Texas protest and encouraged both sides to battle in the streets." In *Business Insider*, November 1, 2017. https://www.businessinsider.com/russia-trolls-senate-intelligence-committee-hearing-2017-11

Billig, Michael. *Banal Nationalism*. London, 1995.

Bishop, Claire. *Artificial Hells: Participatory Art and the Politics of Spectatorship*. London, 2012.

Blackwell, Mark, quoted from Gabbard, Christopher D. "From Idiot Beast to Idiot Sublime: Mental Disability in John Cleland's 'Fanny Hill.'" In *PMLA* 123, no. 2, 2008.

Blanc, Jarrett. "Here's Why World Leaders Are Laughing at Trump." In *Politico*, September 25, 2018. https://www.politico.com/magazine/story/2018/09/25/donald-trump-un-speech-laughing-unga-iran-220620/

Bloch, Ernst. *The Principle of Hope* (1959). Vol. 1. Trans. Neville Plaice et al. Cambridge, 1995.

Bobbitt, Philip. *The Shield of Achilles*. New York, 2003.

Böhmer, Otto A. "Genius c. t." In *ZEIT Campus 06/2008*, November 13, 2008. https://www.zeit.de/campus/2008/06/friedrich-hegel/komplettansicht

Bordiga, Amadeo. "Janitzio Death is not Scary." Trans. Conor Murray. In *Il Programma Comunista*, December 23, 1961. https://www.marxists.org/archive/bordiga/works/1961/janitzio.htm

Bourdieu, Pierre. *Über das Fernsehen*. Frankfurt, 1998.

Brassier, Ray. *Nihil Unbound. Enlightenment and Extinction*. London, 2007.

Braudel, Fernand. *Afterthoughts on Material Civilization and Capitalism*. Trans. Patricia Ranum. Baltimore, 1977.

Brock, Bazon. *Ästhetik als Vermittlung. Arbeitsbiographie eines Generalisten*. Cologne, 1977.

— *Der Barbar als Kulturheld*. Cologne, 2002.

— *Bauhaus-Programm heute: Widerruf des 20. Jahrhunderts*. Cologne, 2001.

Büchner, Georg. *The Complete Works and Letters*. Trans. Walter Hinderer, Henry J. Schmidt. New York, 1986.

Bukowski, Charles. *The Last Night of the Earth Poems*. Boston, 1992.

Buiter, Willem H. "Lessons from the global financial crisis for regulators and supervisors." In *Financial Markets Group Discussion Papers DP 635*, July 2009. https://www.fmg.ac.uk/publications/discussion-papers/lessons-global-financial-crisis-regulators-and-supervisors

Burkeman, Oliver. "How the news took over reality." In *The Guardian*, May 3, 2019. https://www.theguardian.com/news/2019/may/03/how-the-news-took-over-reality

Camatte, Jacques. *Das Buch gegen den Tod*. Munich, 2014.

— "Glossaire." https://revueinvariance.pagesperso-orange.fr/glossaire.html

— *This World We Must Leave and Other Essays*. New York, 1995.

Canetti, Elias. *Crowds and Power*. Trans. Carol Stewart. New York, 1962.

Cavell, Stanley. *Die Unheimlichkeit des Gewöhnlichen*. Frankfurt, 2000.

Chekhov, Anton. "A Happy Man." In *The Horse Stealers and Other Stories*. Trans. Constance Garnet. Project Gutenberg, 2018.

Chesterton, G.K. "The Hammer of God." In *The Innocence of Father Brown*. London, New York, 1911.

Chomsky, Noam. "Trump in the White House." Interview in *Truthout*, November 14, 2016. https://truthout.org/articles/trump-in-the-white-house-an-interview-with-noam-chomsky/

Cioran, Emil. *Vom Nachteil, geboren zu sein. Gedanken und Aphorismen*. Frankfurt, 1979.

Cipolla, Carlo M. *The Basic Laws of Human Stupidity*. Bologna, 2011.

Closky, Claude. *The first thousand numbers classified in alphabetical order*. Self-published,1989. http://ww.closky.info

Collins, Jeremy. "'The facts don't work': The EU referendum campaign and the journalistic construction of 'Post-truth politics.'" In *Discourse, Context & Media* 253, 2018. https://doi.org/10.1016/j.dcm.2018.04.009

Combes, Muriel. *Gilbert Simondon and the Philosophy of the Transindividual*. Cambridge, 2012.

Corazzol, Martina et al. "Restoring consciousness with vagus nerve stimulation." In *Current Biology* 27, no. 18, 2017. https://doi.org/10.1016/j.cub.2017.07.060

Critchley, Simon. *Infinitely Demanding: Ethics of Commitment, Politics of Resistance*. London, 2007.

Curtis, Neal. *Idiotism, Captialism and the Privatization of Life*. London, 2013.

Cusa, Nicholas of. *On Learned Ignorance*. Trans. Jaspar Hopkins. Minneapolis, 1985.

— *On Wisdom and Knowledge*. Trans. Jaspar Hopkins. Minneapolis, 1996.

Dale, Daniel. "'Sir' alert: This one word is a telltale sign Trump is being dishonest." In *CNN*, July 17, 2019. https://edition.cnn.com/2019/07/16/politics/sir-trump-telltale-word-false/index.html

Davies, William. "Why we stopped trusting elites." In *The Guardian*, November 28, 2018. https://www.theguardian.com/news/2018/nov/29/why-we-stopped-trusting-elites-the-new-populism

Debord, Guy. *Society of the Spectacle*. Trans. Ken Knabb. London, 2005.

Debray, Régis. *Jenseits der Bilder. Eine Geschichte der Bildbetrachtung im Abendland*. Rodenbach, 2007.

Deleuze, Gilles. *Difference and Repetition*. Trans. Paul Patton. New York, 1994.

— "Letter to a Harsh Critic." In *Negotiations*. New York, 1995

— "Seminar on Spinoza." February 2, 1980. Quoted from Han, Byung-Chul. *Psychopolitics. Neoliberalism and New Technology*. London, 2017.

— & Félix Guattari. *What is Philosophy?* Trans. Hugh Tomlinson and Graham Burchell. New York, 1994.

DeLillo, Don. *Cosmopolis*. New York, 2003.

— *Mao II*. New York, 1992.

— *Underworld*. New York, 1997.

Demirović, Alex. *Der nonkonformistische Intellektuelle. Die Entwicklung der Kritischen Theorie zur Frankfurter Schule*. Frankfurt, 1999.

Descartes, René. *Descartes' philosophische Werke I–III*. Berlin, 1870.

Desmond, William. *God and the Inbetween*. Hoboken, 2008.

— "The Idiocy of Being in Aquinas' Third Way." Thomas Lecture, Saint Meinrad Seminary and School of Theology, April 6, 2017. https:// www.youtube.com/watch?v=g7sJswuzO2g&t=4s

— "Idiot Wisdom and the Intimate Universal. On Immanence and Transcendence in an Intercultural Perspective." In Brown, N. & W. Franke, eds. *Transcendence, Immanence, and Intercultural Philosophy*. London, 2016.

Diderot, Denis. *Thoughts on the Interpretation of Nature and Other Philosophical Works*. Trans. Lorna Sadler. Manchester, 2000.

Dijksterhuis, Ap et al. "On making the right choice. The deliberation-without-attention effect." In *Science* 311, no. 5763, February 17, 2006. https://www.researchgate.net/publication/7291642_On_Making_the_Right_Choice_The_Deliberation-Without-Attention_Effect

Dirle, Stephen. *Onan the Illiterate.* New York, 2007. http://ubu.com/ubu/unpub/Unpub_006_Dirle_Onan.pdf

Dolar, Mladen. *A Voice and Nothing More.* Cambridge, 2006.

Dolnick, Sam. "The Man Who Knew Too Little." In *The New York Times*, March 10, 2018. https://www.nytimes.com/2018/03/10/style/the-man-who-knew-too-little.html

Dostoyevsky, Fyodor. *The Idiot* (1868). Trans. Alan Myers. Oxford, 1992.

Down, J. Langdon. *On Some of the Mental Affections of Childhood and Youth.* London, 1887.

Driesen, Christian. "Wie Deleuze den Idioten gibt." In *Zeitschrift für Ideengeschichte* IV/2, 2010.

Dürrenmatt, Friedrich. *Selected Writings.* Vol. 1, *Plays.* Trans. Joel Agee. Chicago, 2006.

Dupuy, Jean-Pierre. *Economy and the Future.* Chicago, 2014.

Dutton, Kevin. *Psychopathen: Was man von Heiligen, Anwälten und Serienmördern lernen kann.* Munich, 2013.

Ehrenberg, Alain. *The Weariness of the Self: Diagnosing the History of Depression in the Contemporary Age.* Trans. David Homel et al. Montreal, 2010.

Engels, Friedrich. "On Anti-Semitism." In *Karl Marx and Frederick Engels Correspondence 1846–1895.* London, 1934. https://www.marxists.org/archive/marx/works/1890/04/19.htm

— *Anti-Dühring. Herr Eugen Dühring's Revolution in Science.* marxists.org, 1996. https://www.marxists.org/archive/marx/works/1877/anti-duhring/index.htm

— *The Origin of the Family, Private Property and the State.* marxists.org, 2021. https://www.marxists.org/archive/marx/works/1884/origin-family/index.htm

Enzensberger, Hans Magnus. *Im Irrgarten der Intelligenz. Ein Idiotenführer.* Frankfurt, 2007.

Erasmus, *In Praise of Folly* (1509). Trans. John Wilson (1668). Oxford, 1913.

Erikson, Erik. *Childhood and Society* (1951). London, 1987.

Escobar, Pepe. "Welcome to the Jungle." In *Consortium News*, October 29, 2018. https://consortiumnews.com/2018/10/29/welcome-to-the-jungle

Esquirol, Jean-Etienne-Dominique. *Die Geisteskrankheiten in Beziehung zur Medizin und Staatsarzneikunde.* Vol. 2. Berlin, 1838.

Fanon, Frantz. *Alienation and Freedom.* Trans. Steven Corcoran. London, 2018.

Faulkner, William. "An Introduction to *The Sound and The Fury.*" In *Mississippi Quarterly* 26, 1973.

— *The Sound and The Fury.* New York, 2011.

Feyerabend, Paul. *Wider den Methodenzwang.* Frankfurt, 1976.

Feynman, Richard. *The Meaning of it All*. Boston, 1963.

Flaubert, Gustave & George Sand. *The George Sand–Gustave Flaubert Letters*. Trans. A.L. McKenzie. Project Gutenberg, 2002.

Fleischhauer, Jan. "Narzissmus und Politik." In *Spiegel Online*, October 24, 2016. http://www.spiegel.de/politik/ausland/narzissmus-und-politik-heulsusen-alarm-kolumne-a-1117993.html

Flynn, Meagan. "Hipsters all look the same, man inadvertently confirms." In *Washington Post*, March 7, 2019. https://www.washingtonpost.com/nation/2019/03/07/hipsters-all-look-same-man-inadvertently-confirms/

Foucault, Michel. *History of Madness* (1972). Trans. Jonathan Murphy, Jean Khalfa. London, New York, 2006.

— *Security, Territory, Population. Lectures at the Collège de France, 1977–1978*. Trans. Graham Burchell. New York, 2007.

Frankfurt, Harry G. *On Bullshit*. Princeton, 2005.

Frank, Manfred. *Ansichten der Subjektivität*. Frankfurt, 2012.

Fraser, Nancy. "From Progressive Neoliberalism to Trump." In *American Affairs* 4, winter 2017.

Freeman, Hadley. "From New York's fake heiress to Donald Trump, we're living in the age of the scam." In *The Guardian,* May 11, 2019.

Freud, Sigmund. *Zur Einführung des Narzissmus*. Leipzig, 1924.

Frey, Carl Benedikt. *The Technology Trap. Capital, Labor, and Power in the Age of Automation*. Princeton, 2019.

Friedell, Egon. *Kulturgeschichte der Neuzeit. Die Krisis der europäischen Seele von der schwarzen Pest bis zum Weltkrieg*. 3 vols. Munich, 2011.

Fromm, Erich. *The Anatomy of Human Destructiveness*. New York, 1973.

Garrabé, Jean. "Nosographie et classifications des maladies mentales dans l'histoire de la psychiatrie." In *L'Évolution psychiatrique* 79, 2014.

Geuss, Raymond. *A World Without Why*. Princeton, 2014.

Gibson, William. *Pattern Recognition*. New York, 2003.

Glaser, Jack & John F. Kihlstrom. "Compensatory Automaticity: Unconscious Volition Is Not an Oxymoron." In Hasin, Ran R. et al. *The New Unconscious*. Oxford, 2005.

Goethe, J. W. *Italian Journey*. Trans. W. H. Auden and Elizabeth Mayer (1962). London, 1970.

Goodhart, David. *The Road to Somewhere. The Populist Revolt and the Future of Politics*. London, 2017.

Goodwin, James S. et al. "Association of Chronic Opioid Use With Presidential Voting Patterns in US Counties in 2016," In *JAMA Network Open*, June 22, 2018. https://jamanetwork.com/journals/jamanetworkopen/fullarticle/2685627

Gould, Stephen Jay. *The Mismeasure of Man*. New York, 1996.

Gregory, Leland. *Hey Idiot! Chronicles of Human Stupidity*. Kansas City, 2003.

Graeber, David. *Bullshit Jobs: A Theory.* New York, 2018.

— "On the Phenomenon of Bullshit Jobs: A Work Rant." In *Printed* 3, August 2013. http://www.strikemag.org/bullshit-jobs/

Greenspan, Stephen. "Intelligence and Stupid Behavior. Non-cognitive contributors to irrationality." In *Psychology Today*, November 2, 2016.

Greenfield, Adam. *Radical Technologies.* London, New York, 2017.

Groom, Winston. *Forrest Gump.* New York, 1999.

Gruen, Arno. *Der Wahnsinn der Normalität. Realismus als Krankheit. Eine Theorie der menschlichen Destruktivität.* Munich, 1992.

Gründel, Johannes. "Kairos." In *Lexikon für Theologie und Kirche.* Vol. 5. Freiburg im Breisgau, 1996.

Guattari, Félix. "Capital as the integral of Power Formations." In Guattari, Félix. *Soft Subversions: Texts and Interviews 1977–1985.* Ed. Sylvère Lotringer. Los Angeles, 2009

— *Chaosmosis. An Ethico-Aesthetic Paradigm.* Trans. Paul Bains and Julian Pefanis. Bloomington, 1995.

— "A New Alliance Is Possible." In Guattari, Félix. *Soft Subversions: Texts and Interviews 1977–1985.* Ed. Sylvère Lotringer. Los Angeles, 2009.

— *Planetarischer Kapitalismus.* Berlin, 2018.

Habermas, Jürgen. *The Postnational Constellation: Political Essays* (1998). Trans. Max Pensky. Cambridge, 2001.

Halliwell, Martin. *Images of Idiocy. The Idiot Figure in Modern Fiction and Film.* Abingdon, 2004.

Han, Byung-Chul. *In the Swarm: Digital Prospects.* Cambridge, 2017.

— *Psychopolitics. Neoliberalism and New Technology.* London, 2017.

Handke, Peter. *Der Rand der Wörter.* Stuttgart, 1975.

— *Das Spiel vom Fragen oder Die Reise zum sonoren Land.* Frankfurt, 1989.

Handke, Peter & André Müller. "Wer einmal versagt im Schreiben, hat für immer versagt." Interview in *Die Zeit*, March 3, 1989. https://www.zeit.de/1989/10/wer-einmal-versagt-im-schreiben-hat-fuer-immer-versagt/komplettansicht

Harari, Yuval Noah. *21 Lektionen für das 21. Jahrhundert.* Munich, 2018.

Harrebye, Silas F. *Social Change and Creative Activism in the 21st Century.* London, 2016.

Harvey, David. *Marx, Capital and the Madness of Economic Reason.* Oxford, 2017.

Haug, Wolfgang Fritz. *Jean-Paul Sartre und die Konstruktion des Absurden.* Frankfurt, 1966.

Hauptmann, Gerhart. *The Fool In Christ: Emmanuel Quint* (1910). Trans. Thomas Seltzer. Whitefish, 2010.

Hegel, Georg Wilhelm Friedrich. *Phenomenology of Spirit* (1807). Trans. Terry Pinkard. Cambridge, 2018.

Heidegger, Martin. *Discourse on Thinking*. Trans. John M. Anderson and E. Hans Freund. New York, 1966.

— *Über den Anfang* (1943). Vol. 70 of *Gesamtausgabe*. Frankfurt, 2005.

— *Überlegungen XII–XV (Schwarze Hefte 1939–1941)*. Vol. 96 of *Gesamtausgabe*. Frankfurt, 2005.

Heller, Nathan. "The Bullshit-Job Boom." In *The New Yorker*, June 7, 2018. https://www.newyorker.com/books/under-review/the-bullshit-job-boom

Hendrikse, Reijer & Rodrigo Fernandez. "Offshore Finance: How Capital Rules the World." In *TNI Longreads*, January 2019. http://longreads.tni.org/state-of-power-2019/offshore-finance/

Höge, Helmut. "Schafe haben Meinungen," In *TAZ Online*, May 26, 2019. https://taz.de/Tiere-in-Europa/!5594851/

Hölderlin, Friedrich. *Selected Poetry*. Trans. David Constantine. Hexham, 2018.

Howard, Dick. *The Primacy of the Political: A History of Political Thought from the Greeks to the French and American Revolutions*. New York, 2013.

Huyssen, Andreas & Klaus Scherpe, eds. *Postmoderne. Zeichen eines kulturellen Wandels*. Reinbek bei Hamburg, 1989.

Hyde, Lewis. *Trickster Makes this World. Mischief, Myth, and Art*. New York, 1998.

Illing, Sean. "Bullshit jobs: why they exist and why you might have one." In *Vox*, May 8, 2018. https://www.vox.com/2018/5/8/17308744/bullshit-jobs-book-david-graeber-occupy-wall-street-karl-marx

Illouz, Eva. *Cold Intimacies: The Making of Emotional Capitalism*. Cambridge, 2007.

— "Warum haben die Menschen immer weniger Sex?" In *Tagesspiegel Online*, June 7, 2019. https://m.tagesspiegel.de/gesellschaft/interview-mit-eva-illouz-warum-haben-die-menschen-immer-weniger-sex/24376458.html

Ionesco, Eugène. "Dans les armes de la ville." In *Cahiers de la Compagnie Madeleine Renaud-Jean-Louis Barrault* 20, October 1957. Quoted from Esslin, Martin. *The Theatre of the Absurd* (1961). London, 2001.

Jacobs, David. *At Dusk. The Situationist Movement in Historical Perspective*. Berkeley, 1975.

Jacoby, Suzan. *The Age of American Unreason in a Culture of Lies*. New York, 2018.

Jameson, Fredric. *The Cultural Turn. Selected Writings on the Postmodern 1983–1998*. London, New York, 1998.

— *The Hegel Variations*. London, New York, 2010.

— *The Political Unconscious. Narrative as a Socially Symbolic Act*. Cornell, 1996.

— *Postmodernism, or, The Cultural Logic of Late Capitalism*. Durham, 1991.

Jarry, Alfred. *König Ubu*. Stuttgart, 1996.

Joffe, Josef. "2 + 2 = 5." In *Die ZEIT Online* 6, February 2, 2017. https://www.zeit.de/2017/06/1984-george-orwell-donald-trump-verstehen-zeitgeist

Kafka, Franz. *The Trial.* Trans. Mike Mitchell. Oxford, 2009.

— *The Blue Octavo Notebooks* (1917). Ed. Max Brod. Trans. Ernst Kaiser, Eithne Wilkins. Cambridge, 1991.

Kahneman, Daniel. *Thinking. Fast and Slow.* New York, 2011.

Kahn-Harris, Keith. "Denialism: what drives people to reject the truth." In *The Guardian*, August 3, 2018. https://www.theguardian.com/news/2018/aug/03/denialism-what-drives-people-to-reject-the-truth

Kant, Immanuel. *Grundlegung zur Metaphysik der Sitten.* Vol. 7 of the collected works in 12 vols., Frankfurt, 1977.

— *Kritik der reinen Vernunft.* Vol. 3. of the collected works in 12 vols. Frankfurt, 1977.

Karnie, Anne. "Trump's assault on Woodward riddled with contradictions." In *Politico*, October 28, 2018.

Kellershohn, Helmut, ed. *"Die Deutsche Stimme" der "Jungen Freiheit." Lesarten des völkischen Nationalismus in zentralen Publikationen der extremen Rechten.* Münster, 2013.

Kertesz, Imre. *Fatelessness.* Trans. Tim Wilkinson. New York, 2004.

Keynes, John Maynard. *Essays in Persuasion.* New York, 1963.

Kierkegaard, Søren. *Entweder-Oder. Ein Lebensfragment.* Leipzig, 1885.

King, Josh. "Trump's big league microphone. A golden gooseneck." In *The Verge*, January 25, 2017. https://www.theverge.com/2017/1/25/14384774/trump-microphone-speech-long-neck-shure-sm57

Kompridis, Nikolas. "The idea of a new beginning. A romantic source of normativity and freedom." In Nikolas Kompridis, ed. *Philosophical Romanticism.* Abingdon, 2006.

—, ed. *Philosophical Romanticism.* Abingdon, 2006.

Knausgård, Karl Ove & Jesse Barron. "Completely Without Dignity: An Interview with Karl Ove Knausgaard." In *The Paris Review*, December 26, 2013. https://www.theparisreview.org/blog/2013/12/26/completely-without-dignity-an-interview-with-karl-ove-knausgaard/

Kraus, Karl. *Polemiken, Glossen, Verse und Szenen.* Leipzig, 1987.

Kron, Thomas & Melanie Reddig. "Zygmunt Bauman: Die ambivalente Verfassung moderner und postmoderner Kultur." In Moebius, S. & D. Quadflieg, eds. *Kultur: Theorien der Gegenwart.* Wiesbaden, 2006.

Kruse, Michael. "1988: The Year Donald Lost His Mind." In *Politico Magazine*, March 11, 2016. https://www.politico.com/magazine/story/2016/03/1988-the-year-donald-lost-his-mind-213721/

Küpper, Christian. "'Psychologie reicht ans Grauen nicht heran' – Adorno zu Individuum und Gesellschaft." In *Forum Kritische Psychologie* 53, 2009. https://www.kritische-psychologie.de/files/FKP_53_Christian_Küpper.pdf

Kurzweil, Ray. *The Singularity Is Near.* New York, 2005.

— "Technology Will Achieve the Goals of Communism." Interview at The World Technology Network – TIME Conference Center, 2012. https://www.dailymotion.com/video/xvmcob

— "Waking the universe." Interview in *somethinkblue*, May 1, 2011. https://www.kurzweilai.net/waking-the-universe

Lacan, Jacques. *The Seminar, Book IX. Identification. 1961–1962.* London, 2002. http://www.lacaninireland.com/web/wp-content/uploads/2010/06/Seminar-IX-Amended-Iby-MCL-7.NOV_.20111.pdf

— *Das Seminar, Buch X. Die Angst. 1962–1963.* Vienna, 2010.

Laclau, Ernesto. *On Populist Reason.* New York, 2005.

Lacy, Sarah. "Venture Capital and the Great Big Silicon Valley Asshole Game." In *Pando Quarterly* 3, 2014.

Lasch, Christopher. *The Culture of Narcissism.* New York, 1979.

Laska, Bernd A. *Ein dauerhafter Dissident. Wirkungsgeschichte von Max Stirners "Einzigem."* Nuremberg, 1986.

— "'Der ,Eigner' bei Max Stirner." In Laska, Bernd A. *"Katechon" und "Anarch." Carl Schmitts und Ernst Jüngers Reaktionen auf Max Stirner.* Nuremberg, 1997.

— "Die Negation des irrationalen Über-Ichs bei Max Stirner." In *LSR*, 1991. http://www.lsr-projekt.de/msnega.html

Lee, Bandy X., ed. *The Dangerous Case of Donald Trump. 37 Psychiatrists and Mental Health Experts Assess a President.* New York, 2019.

Lefebvre, Henri. *Critique of Everyday Life.* Vols. 1–3. Trans. John Moore. London, New York, 2014.

Leland, Gregory. *Hey Idiot! Chronicles of Human Stupidity.* Kansas City, 2003.

Levitt, Steven D. & Stephen J. Dubner. *Think Like a Freak.* New York, 2014.

Locke, John. *Essay Concerning Human Understanding* (1690). Ed. Peter Nidditch. Oxford, 1975.

Loseff, Lev. "Dostoevsky & 'Don Quixote.'" In *The New York Review of Books*, November 19, 1998. https://www.nybooks.com/articles/1998/11/19/dostoevsky-don-quixote/

Lynn, Barry C. *Cornered. The New Monopoly Capitalism and the Economics of Destruction.* Hoboken, 2010.

Maclagan, David. *Outsider Art. From the Margins to the Marketplace.* London, 2009.

Mann, Thomas. *Doktor Faustus.* Frankfurt, 2001.

Marchart, Oliver. *Neu beginnen. Hannah Arendt, die Revolution und die Globalisierung.* Vienna, 2005.

Marcuse, Herbert. *One-Dimensional Man* (1964). Abingdon, New York, 2007.

Marshall, Eric and Stuart Hample. *Children's Letters to God.* New York, 1991.

Martin, Bruno. *Der verwirklichte Idiot. Die kunstvolle Psychologie von G.I. Gurdjieff.* BoD, 2013.

Marx, Karl. *Capital.* marxists.org, 1995/99. https://www.marxists.org/archive/marx/works/1867-c1/index.htm

— *The Poverty of Philosophy.* marxists.org, 2009. https://www.marxists.org/archive/marx/works/1847/poverty-philosophy/index.htm

— & Friedrich Engels. *Manifesto of the Communist Party.* marxists.org, 2000. https://www.marxists.org/archive/marx/works/1848/communist-manifesto/

Matheson, Rob. "Inventing the 'Google' for predictive analytics." In *MIT News*, December 19, 2017. https://news.mit.edu/2017/endor-inventing-google-predictive-analytics-1220

Maurer, Friedrich et al. *Deutsche Wortgeschichte.* Vol. 2. Berlin, 1959.

Mbembe, Achille. *Critique of Black Reason.* Trans. Laurent Dubois. Durham, London, 2017.

McDonagh, Patrick. *Idiocy: A Cultural History.* Liverpool, 2008.

— *The Image of Idiocy in Nineteenth-century England: A History of Cultural Representations of Intellectual Disability.* Montreal, 1998.

— et al., eds. *Intellectual Disability. A Conceptual History, 1200–1900.* Manchester, 2018.

McDonough, Tom. "Rereading Debord, Rereading the Situationists." In *October Magazine* 79, winter 1997. https://fdocuments.in/document/october-20121001-october-79-winter-1997-pp-3-14-1997-october-magazine.html

Meillasoux, Quentin. *Trassierungen. Zur Wegbereitung spekulativen Denkens.* Berlin, 2017.

*Meyers Großes Konversations-Lexikon.* Vol. 5. Leipzig, 1906.

Mettrie, Julien de La. *Man a Machine* (1995). Trans. Mitch Abidor. marxists.org, 2006. https://www.marxists.org/reference/archive/la-mettrie/1748/man-machine.htm

Metz, Markus & Georg Seeßlen. *Blödmaschinen.* Frankfurt, 2011.

Metzger, Gustav. "Auto-Destructive Art Manifesto" (1960). UbuWeb. https://www.ubu.com/papers/metzger_auto-destructive.html

Metzinger, Thomas. *Der Ego-Tunnel.* Munich, 2014.

Mezzadra, Sandro. "What's at Stake in the Mobility of Labour? Borders, Migration, Contemporary Capitalism." In *Migration, Mobility & Displacement* 2 (1). Durham, 2016.

Michaux, Henri. *Miserable Miracle* (1963). Trans. Louise Varèse. New York, 2002.

Mirowski, Philip. *Machine Dreams: Economics Becomes a Cyborg Science.* Cambridge, 2001.

— *More Heat than Light. Economics as Social Physics, Physics as Nature's Economics.* Cambridge, 1989.

Mitroff, Ian I. & Warren G. Bennis. *The Unreality Industry: The Deliberate Manufacturing of Falsehood and What It Is Doing to Our Lives.* New York, Oxford, 1993.

Monbiot, George. "Killer Clowns." In *The Guardian*, July 29, 2019. https://www.monbiot.com/2019/07/30/killer-clowns/

— "Neoliberalism is Creating Loneliness. That's What's Wrenching Society Apart." In *The Guardian*, October 12, 2016. https://www.theguardian.com/commentisfree/2016/oct/12/neoliberalism-creating-loneliness-wrenching-society-apart

Morillas, Antonio & Jordi Morillas. "Der 'Idiot' bei Nietzsche und Dostojewskij. Geschichte eines Irrtums." In *Nietzsche-Studien* 41, no. 1, 2012. doi:10.1515/ niet.2012.41.1.344

Morris, Steven. "'Banksy of punctuation' puts full stop to bad grammar in Bristol." In *The Guardian*, April 3, 2017. https://www.theguardian.com/education/2017/apr/03/banksy-of-punctuation-puts-full-stop-bad-grammar-bristol

Mühlmann, Heiner. *Die Natur der Kulturen*. Munich, 2011.

Müller, Heiner. "Es gibt ein Menschenrecht auf Feigheit." Interview by Thomas Assheuer in *Frankfurter Rundschau*, May 22, 1993. Also in *Werke*, vol. 12. Frankfurt, 2008.

Müller, Wolfgang, ed. *Geniale Dilletanten*. Berlin, 1981.

— "Geniale Dilletanten." In *Glossar inflationärer Begriffe*, Berlin, 2013.

Münkler, Herfried. "Vom Verlust des revolutionären Subjekts. Die politische Dimension moderer und postmoderner Ästhetiken." In Münkler, Herfried & Richard Saage, eds. *Kultur und Politik. Brechungen der Fortschrittsperspektive heute*. Opladen, 1989.

Münkler, Herfried & Richard Saage, eds. *Kultur und Politik. Brechungen der Fortschrittsperspektive heute*. Opladen, 1989.

Musil, Robert. *The Man Without Qualities*. Vols. 1 and 2. Trans. Sophie Wilkins. New York, 1996.

— *Über Dummheit*. Frankfurt, 1978.

Nagel, Alexander. "Twenty-five notes on pseudoscript in Italian art." In *RES* 59/60, spring/autumn 2011. https://ifa.nyu.edu/people/faculty/nagel_PDFs/Nagel_final.pdf

Nagel, Thomas. "The Absurd." In *The Journal of Philosophy*. Vol. 68, no. 20, October 21, 1971.

Nagle, Angela. "The Left Case against Open Borders." In *American Affairs* 2, no. 4, winter 2018. https://americanaffairsjournal.org/2018/11/the-left-case-against-open-borders/

Nancy, Jean-Luc. *The Birth to Presence*. Palo Alto, 1993.

— *The Inoperative Community*. Trans. Peter Connor. Minneapolis, Oxford, 1991

— *The Sense of the World* (1993). Trans. Jeffrey S. Librett. Minneapolis, London, 1997.

— *Was tun?* Zurich, Berlin, 2017

— "What is To Be Done." Trans. Irving Goh. In *diacritics* 42, no. 2, 2014. https://muse.jhu.edu/article/576042.

Negri, Antonio & Michael Hardt. *Empire*. Cambridge, London 2000.

Nietzsche, Friedrich. *The Anti-Christ, Ecce Homo, Twilight of the Idols and Other Writings*. Ed. Aaron Ridley. Trans. Judith Norman. Cambridge, 2005

— "Die fröhliche Wissenschaft." In *Werke in drei Bänden*. Vol 2. Munich, 1954.

— "Jenseits von Gut und Böse." In *Werke in drei Bänden*. Vol 2. Munich, 1954.

— *Last Notebooks* (1888). Trans. Daniel Fidel Ferrer. Online 2012. https://philarchive.org/archive/FERNLN

— *Die nachgelassenen Fragmente*. Stuttgart, 1996.

— "Die Philosophie im tragischen Zeitalter der Griechen." In *Werke in drei Bänden*. Vol. 3. Munich, 1954.

— *Thus Spoke Zarathustra* (1883–85). Trans. Thomas Common. Paris, 2010.

— *The Will to Power*. Trans. Walter Kaufmann, R.J. Hollingdale. New York, 1967.

— "Über Wahrheit und Lüge im außermoralischen Sinn." In *Werke in drei Bänden*. Vol. 3. Munich, 1954.

Nozick, Robert. *Anarchy, State and Utopia*. Hoboken, 2001.

O'Connor, Flannery. *Wise Blood*. New York, 2007.

Onfray, Michel. *A Hedonist Manifesto—the Power to Exist*. New York, 2015.

Ortega y Gasset, José. *The Revolt of the Masses*. Trans. J.R. Carey. New York, 1932.

— "Warum die Massen in alles eingreifen und warum sie mit Gewalt ein- greifen." Quoted from Walter, Lutz. *Lob der Dummheit*. Stuttgart, Leipzig, 2000.

Orwell, George. "Politics and the English Language." In *In All Art is Propaganda: Critical Essays*. Ed. George Packer. Boston, New York, 2008.

Osnos, Evan. "Doomsday Prep for the Super-Rich." In *The New Yorker*, January 30, 2017. https://www.newyorker.com/magazine/2017/01/30/doomsday-prep-for-the-super-rich

Page, Martin. *How I Became Stupid*. Trans. Adriana Hunter. London, 2004.

Panizza, Oskar. *Genie und Wahnsinn*. e-artnow, 2018.

Parker, Walter C. "Teaching against Idiocy." In *Phi Delta Kappan* 86, no. 5, 2005. https://faculty.washington.edu/rsoder/EDUC305/305parkeridiocy.pdf

Pasolini, Pier Paolo. "Pier Paolo Pasolini Interviewed by Enzo Biagi for the Italian television network RAI." July 27, 1971. https://libcom.org/article/pier-paolo-pasolini-interviewed-enzo-biagi-italian-television-network-rai-july-27-1971

Pasquarelli, Adrianne. "Chase commits to AI after machines outperform humans in copywriting trials." In *AdAge*, July 30, 2019. https://adage.com/article/cmo-strategy/chase-commits-to-ai-after-machines-outperform-humans-copywriting-trials/2187606

Paul, Christopher and Miriam Matthews. "The Russian 'Firehose of Falsehood' Propaganda Model." In *RAND Corporation*, 2016. https://www.rand.org/pubs/perspectives/PE198.html

Penny, Laurie. "Life-Hacks of the Poor and Aimless. On negotiating the false idols of neoliberal self-care." In *The Baffler*, July 8, 2016. https://thebaffler.com/latest/laurie-penny-self-care

Pentland, Alex. *Social Physics. How Good Ideas Spread*. New York, 2014.

— "Society's Nervous System. Building Effective Government, Energy, and Public Health Systems." In *MIT Open Access Articles*, October 2011. http://dspace.mit.edu/handle/1721.1/66256

— "Reality Mining of Mobile Communications. Toward a New Deal on Data." In *The Global Information Technology Report 2008–2009*. World Economic Forum, 2009. https://hd.media.mit.edu/wef_globalit.pdf

Peretti, Luca & Karen Raizen. *Pier Paolo Pasolini, Framed and Unframed: A Thinker for the Twenty-First Century*. London, 2018.

Perrow, Charles. *Normale Katastrophen*. Frankfurt, New York, 1987.

Pessoa, Fernando. *The Book of Disquiet*. Trans. Robert Zenith. London, 2001.

Pesta, Abigail. "Looking for Something Useful to Do With Your Time? Don't Try This." In *The Wall Street Journal*, March 12, 2013. https://www.wsj.com/articles/SB10001424127 887323628804578348572687608806

Pinel, Philippe. *Traité médico-philosophique sur l'aliénation mentale, ou La manie*. Paris, 1801.

Plato. *Laws*. Trans. Benjamin Jowett (1885). Project Gutenberg, 2021. https://www.gutenberg.org/files/1497/1497-h/1497-h.htm

— "Die Verteidigung des Sokrates." In *Sämtliche Werke*. Vol 1. Berlin, 1940.

Pöppel, Ernst & Beatrice Wagner. *Dummheit. Warum wir heute die einfachsten Dinge nicht mehr wissen*. Munich, 2013.

Pohrt, Wolfgang. *Kapitalismus Forever. Über Krise, Krieg, Revolution, Evolution, Christentum und Islam*. Berlin, 2012.

— *Das allerletzte Gefecht. Über den universellen Kapitalismus, den Kommunismus als Episode und die Menschheit als Amöbe*. Bremen, 2013.

Poley, Stefanie, ed. *Unter der Maske des Narren*. Stuttgart, 1981.

Poole, Matthew. "The Idiot Paradigm." In Cox, C. et al., eds. *Realism Materialism Art*. New York, Berlin, 2015.

Porphyry. *Introduction*. Trans. J. Barnes. Oxford, 2006.

Posèq, Avigdor W. G. "The Allegorical Content of Caravaggio's 'Narcissus.'" In *Notes in the History of Art* 10, no. 3, spring 1991. http://www.jstor.org/stable/23203015

Postone, Moishe. *Time, Labor and Social Domination*. Cambridge, 1993.

— *History and Heteronomy*. Tokyo, 2009.

Pynchon, Thomas. *Gravity's Rainbow*. New York, 2006.

— *Against the Day*. New York, 2006.

Rancière, Jacques. *Disagreement. Politics and Philosophy*. Minnesota, 1998.

— *Aufteilung des Sinnlichen*. Berlin, 2006.

— *Chronicles of Consensual Times*. Trans. Steven Corcoran. London, New York, 2010.

Rawls, John. *A Theory of Justice*. Cambridge, 1971.

Reckwitz, Andreas. *The Society of Singularities*. Trans. Valentine A. Pakis. Cambridge, 2020.

Rehmann, Jan. *Theories of Ideology. The Powers of Alienation and Subjection*. Leiden, Boston, 2013.

Reinhardt. Ad. "Art Theory." In *Art International* 4, no. 10, December 1962.

Renger, Almut-Barbara, ed. *Narcissus. Ein Mythos von der Antike bis zum Cyberspace*. Stuttgart. 2002.

Rinck, Monika. *Risiko und Idiotie*. Berlin, 2015.

Ringelnatz, Joachim. *Das Gesamtwerk in sieben Bänden*. Vol. 1, *Gedichte*. Zurich, 1994.

Ritzer, George. *The McDonaldization of Society*. Newbury Park, 1993.

Rogoff, Kenneth. "Wir erleben einen Kulturkampf." In *Handelsblatt* 197, October 13, 2018.

Ronell, Avital. *Stupidity*. Chicago, 2002.

Rosa, Hartmut. *Beschleunigung. Die Veränderung der Zeitstrukturen in der Moderne*. Frankfurt, 2005.

— *Resonanz: Eine Soziologie der Weltbeziehung*. Frankfurt, 2016.

Rosset, Clément. *Das Reale. Traktat über Idiotie*. Frankfurt, 1988.

— *Das Reale in seiner Einzigartigkeit*. Berlin, 2000.

Rubiner, Ludwig. *Der Mensch in der Mitte*. Potsdam, 1920.

Saar, Yuval & Hagit Saad. "Alone Together. We Live with Them and Sleep with Them, But Do We Really and Truly Know Our Mates?" In *Haaretz Online*, February 25, 2011. https://www.haaretz.com/1.5128113

Sacks, Oliver. "The Autist Artist." In *The Man Who Mistook His Wife for a Hat and Other Clinical Tales*. New York, 1985.

Samol, Peter. *All the Lonely People. Narzissmus als adäquate Subjektform des Kapitalismus*. Nuremberg, 2016. https://www.krisis.org/wp-content/data/krisis_4_2016-Samol-all_the_lonely_people.pdf

Sandberg, Anders. "The five biggest threats to human existence." In *The Conversation*, May 29, 2014. https://theconversation.com/the-five-biggest-threats-to-human-existence-27053

Sartre, Jean-Paul. *The Family Idiot: Gustave Flaubert*. Vol. 1. Trans. Carol Cosman. Chicago, 1981.

— *Being and Nothingness. An Essay in Phenomenological Ontology*. Trans. Sarah Richmond. New York, London, 2018.

Saslow, Eli. "'Nothing on this page is real': How lies become truth in online America." In *The Washington Post*, November 17, 2018. https://www.washingtonpost.com/national/nothing-on-this-page-is-real-how-lies-become-truth-in-online-america/2018/11/17/ed-d44cc8-e85a-11e8-bbdb-72fdbf9d4fed_story.html

Schürmann, Reiner. *Broken Hegemonies*. Trans. Reginald Lilly. Bloomington, 2003.

Schumacher, Claude. *Alfred Jarry and Guillaume Apollinaire*. London, 1984.

Scott, David. *Gilbert Simondon's Psychic and Collective Individuation. A Critical Introduction and Guide*. Edinburgh, 2014.

Semuels, Alana. "Are More and More People Working Meaningless Jobs?" In *The New York Times*, June 19, 2018. https://www.nytimes.com/2018/06/26/books/review/david-graeber-bullshit-jobs.html

Sennett, Richard. *The Fall of Public Man* (1977). London, 2002.

— *The Culture of the New Capitalism*. New Haven, 2006.

Shakespeare, William. *Sämtliche Werke in vier Bänden*. Berlin, 1975.

Shatskikh, Aleksandra. "Inscribed Vandalism: The Black Square at One Hundred." In *e-flux Journal* 85, October 2017. https://www.e-flux.com/journal/85/155475/inscribed-vandalism-the-black-square-at-one-hundred/

Shiller, Robert. *Irrational Exuberance*. Princeton, 2015.

Silesius, Angelus. *Sämtliche poetische Werke in drei Bänden*. Vol. 3. Munich, 1952.

Simic, Charles. "A Year in Fragments." In *The New York Review of Books*, December 31, 2012. https://www.nybooks.com/daily/2012/12/31/year-fragments/

Slobodian, Quinn. *Globalists*. Cambridge, 2018.

Sloterdijk, Peter. *Critique of Cynical Reason*. Trans. Michael Eldred. Minneapolis, 1987.

Sommer, Andreas Urs. "Kurze Geistesgeschichte des Idioten." In *Zeitschrift für Ideengeschichte* 4, no. 2, summer 2010. https://www.z-i-g.de/pdf/ZIG_2_2010_sommer.pdf

Sorabji, Richard. *The Philosophy of the Commentators, 200–600 AD. Logic and Metaphysics*. Ithaca, 2005.

Sørensen, Majken Jul. *Humour in Political Activism. Creative Nonviolent Resistance*. London, 2016.

Sperber, Eliot. "Hey Idiot." In *Counterpunch*, April 10, 2013. https://www.counterpunch.org/2013/04/10/hey-idiot/

Stanovich, Keith E. *What Intelligence Tests Miss: The Psychology of Rational Thought*. New Haven, 2009.

St. Clair, Jeffrey. "The Idiot's Tale: Signifying What, Exactly?" In *Counterpunch*, July 14, 2017. https://www.counterpunch.org/2017/07/14/the-idiots-tale-signifying-what/

Stiegler, Bernard. *Acting Out*. Stanford, 2009.

— *The Decadence of Industrial Democracies. Disbelief and Discredit*. Vol. 1. Cambridge, 2011.

— *The Neganthropocene*. London, 2018.

— *Technics and Time*. Vol. 1, *The Fault of Epimetheus*. Trans. Richard Beardsworth and George Collins. Stanford, 1998.

Stiles, Noelle R. B. et al. "What You Saw Is What You Will Hear: Two New Illusions with Audiovisual Postdictive Effects." In *PLoS ONE* 13, no. 10, 2018. https://journals.plos.org/plosone/article?id=10.1371/journal.pone.0204217

Stirner, Max. *The Ego and its Own* (1907). Ed. David Leopold. Cambridge, 1995.

Strauß, Botho. *Lichter des Toren. Der Idiot und seine Zeit*. Munich, 2013.

— *Beginnlosigkeit. Reflexionen über Fleck und Linie*. Munich, 1997.

Streeck, Wolfgang. *How Will Capitalism End? Essays on a Failing System*. Brooklyn, 2016.

Struck, Lothar. "Der Schriftsteller als Idiot bei Peter Handke und Botho Strauß." In *Handke-online*, April 29, 2014. https://handkeonline.onb.ac.at/forschung/pdf/struck-2014.pdf

Sturgeon, Theodore. *More Than Human*. London, 2000.

Sunstein, Cass R. "Why Free Markets Make Fools of Us." In *The New York Review of Books*, October 22, 2015. https://www.nybooks.com/articles/2015/10/22/why-free-markets-make-fools-us/

Sutter, Laurent de. *Narcocapitalism. Life in the Age of Anaesthesia*. Cambridge, 2018.

Sutton, Robert I. *The No Asshole Rule: Building a Civilized Workplace and Surviving One That Isn't.* New York, 2007.

Taleb, Nassim Nicholas. "Die Wohlwissenden. Die Rebellion gegen den Intellektuellen-Idioten hat eben erst begonnen." In *NZZ*, November 15, 2016. https://www.nzz.ch/feuilleton/aktuell/nassim-nicholas-taleb-die-wohlwissenden-ld.128349

— *The Black Swan. The Impact of the Highly Improbable.* New York, 2007.

— *Fooled by Randomness. The Hidden Role of Chance in Life and in the Markets.* New York, 2001.

Tamás, G. M. "On Post-Fascism. How Citizenship is Becoming an Exclusive Privilege." In *Boston Review*, summer 2000. http://bostonreview.net/archives/BR25.3/tamas.html

Tamny, John. "Surging Wealth Inequality Is A Happy Sign That Life Is Becoming Much More Convenient." In *Forbes Magazine*, November 11, 2018. https://www.forbes.com/sites/johntamny/2018/11/11/surging-wealth-inequality-is-a-happy-sign-that-life-is-becoming-much-more-convenient/?sh=73ad00c464ca

Thiel, Peter. "The Education of a Libertarian." In *Cato Unbound. A Journal of Debate*, April 13, 2009. https://www.cato-unbound.org/2009/04/13/peter-thiel/education-libertarian/

Tocqueville, Alexis de. *Democracy in America.* Vol. 2. Trans. Henry Reeve. Project Gutenberg, 2006.

Toole, John Kennedy. *Die Verschwörung der Idioten.* Stuttgart, 2011.

Tooze, Adam. "A General Logic of Crisis." In *The London Review of Books* 39, no. 1–5, January 2017. https://www.lrb.co.uk/v39/n01/adam-tooze/a-general-logic-of-crisis

Touboul, Jonathan. "The Hipster Effect – When Anti-Conformists All Look the Same." In *arxiv.org*, February 21, 2019. https://arxiv.org/pdf/1410.8001.pdf

Treffert, Darold A. *Islands of Genius: The Bountiful Mind of the Autistic, Acquired, and Sudden Savant.* London, 2010.

Tzara, Tristan. "Lecture on Dada" (1922) and "Dada Manifesto" (1918). Trans. Robert Motherwell. In Motherwell, Robert, ed. *Dada Painters and Poets* (1951). Cambridge, London. 1981.

— "Mr. AA the Antiphilosopher Has Sent Us This Manifesto." In Mary Ann Caws, ed. *Manifesto. A Century of Isms.* Lincoln, London, 2008.

Ugrešić, Dubravka. *The Culture of Lies.* London, 1998.

Valéry, Paul. *The Art of Poetry.* Trans. Denise Folliot. Princeton, 1985.

— *Selected Writings.* New York, 1950.

— *Ich grase meine Gehirnwiese ab. Paul Valéry und seine verborgenen Cahiers.* Frankfurt, 2016.

Vaneigem, Raoul. *The Revolution of Everyday Life.* London, 2003.

Vargas-Cooper, Natasha. "Feminist Students Protest Feminist Prof for Writing About Feminism." In *Jezebel*, May 29, 2015. https://jezebel.com/feminist-students-protest-feminist-prof-for-writing-abo-1707714321

Verhaeghe, Paul. "Neoliberalism has Brought Out the Worst in Us." In *The Guardian*, September 29, 2018. https://www.theguardian.com/commentisfree/2014/sep/29/neoliberalism-economic-system-ethics-personality-psychopathicsthic

Virno, Paulo. *A Grammar of the Multitude*. Trans. Isabella Bertoletti et al. Los Angeles, 2004.

Vltchek, Andre. "Gadgets Turning Me Into an Idiot!" In *Counterpunch*, August 29, 2014. https://www.counterpunch.org/2014/08/29/gadgets-turning-me-into-an-idiot/

Vogl, Joseph. *Das Gespenst des Kapitals*. Zurich, Berlin, 2010.

Voltaire, *Candide, or Optimism*. Trans. Burton Raffel. New Haven, London, 2005.

Walter, Lutz. *Lob der Dummheit*. Stuttgart, Leipzig, 2000.

Warhol, Andy. *The Philosophy of Andy Warhol*. San Diego, 1975.

Waters, Richard. "FT Interview with Google Co-founder and CEO Larry Page." In *Financial Times*, October 20, 2014. https://www.ft.com/content/3173f19e-5fbc-11e4-8c27-00144feabdc0

Weininger, Otto. *On Last Things*. Trans. Steve Burns. Lewiston, 2001.

Welles, James. *A Story of Stupidity*. Greenport, 1988.

Weisberg, Jacob. "The Autocracy App." In *The New York Review of Books*, October 25, 2018. https://www.nybooks.com/articles/2018/10/25/facebook-autocracy-app/

Wertheimer, Jürgen & Peter V. Zima, eds. *Strategien der Verdummung. Infantilisierung in der Fun-Gesellschaft*. Munich, 2006.

Wiener, Oswald & Christian Dany. "Science and barbarism go very well together." Interview in *Spike Magazine* 42, winter 2014.

Winkler, Bernhard. "Der Dichter als Idiot – Zur Poetik des Außenseiters in Botho Strauß' 'Lichter des Toren.'" In *Studia theodisca* XXIII, 2016. https://riviste.unimi.it/index.php/StudiaTheodisca/article/view/7545

Wirth, Uwe. "Dilettantische Konjekturen." In Azzouni & Wirth, eds. *Dilettantismus als Beruf*. Berlin, 2009.

Wittgenstein, Ludwig. *Wiener Ausgabe, Studien Texte*. Vol 3. Frankfurt, 1995.

— *Über Gewissheit*. Frankfurt, 1984.

Witzer, Brigitte. *Die Diktatur der Dummen: Wie unsere Gesellschaft verblödet, weil die Klügeren immer nachgeben*. Munich, 2014.

Wolin, Sheldon. *Tocqueville Between Two Worlds. The Making of a Political and Theoretical Life*. Princeton, 2001.

— *Democracy Incorporated. Managed Democracy and the Specter of Inverted Totalitarianism*. Princeton, 2008.

— *Simulative Demokratie. Neue Politik nach der postdemokratischen Wende*. Berlin, 2013.

Woodward, Bob. *Fear. Trump in the White House*. New York, 2018.

Yago, Dena. "On Ketamine and Added Value." In *e-flux Journal* 82, May, 2017. https://www.e-flux.com/journal/82/133913/on-ketamine-and-added-value/

Zahavi, Dan. *Self-awareness and Alterity. A Phenomenological Investigation*. Evanston, 1999.

— "Being Someone." In *Psyche* 11, no. 5, June 2005. http://journalpsyche.org/files/0xaad8.
    pdf

— *Subjectivity and Selfhood. Investigating the First-Person Perspective*. Cambridge, 2005.

Zänker, Alfred. *Die vielen Gesichter der Dummheit: Torheit – eine Triebfeder des Lebens*. Asend-
    orf, 2001.

Žižek, Slavoj. *Enjoy Your Symptom! Jacques Lacan in Hollywood and out*. Abingdon, 2008.

— *Less than Nothing*. New York, 2013.

— "The Libidinal Economy of Singularity." In *The Philosophical Salon*, August 2019. https://
    thephilosophicalsalon.com/the-libidinal-economy-of-singularity/

— "The Matrix, or, the Two Sides of Perversion." Presentation at *Inside the Matrix*, sympo-
    sium at the Center for Art and Media, Karlsruhe, October 28, 1999. https://www.lacan.
    com/zizek-matrix.htm

Zuboff. Shoshana. *The Age of Surveillance Capitalism: The Fight for a Human Future at the New
    Frontier of Power*. New York, 2019.

© DIAPHANES, Zurich 2022
All rights reserved

ISBN 978-3-0358-0367-9

Layout: 2edit, Zurich
Printed in Germany

www.diaphanes.com